LOST RAILWAYS
OF
SOMERSET

Stan Yorke

COUNTRYSIDE BOOKS

NEWBURY, BERKSHIRE

COUNTRYSIDE BOOKS
3 Catherine Road
Newbury, Berkshire

To view our complete range of books,
please visit us at
www.countrysidebooks.co.uk

ISBN 978 1 84674 057 2

Cover picture shows a class 2P No 40700 with a
local train reaching Masbury Summit, 1959, and
is from an original painting by Colin Doggett

Designed by Mon Mohan

Produced through MRM Associates Ltd., Reading
Typeset by Jean Cussons Typesetting, Diss, Norfolk
Printed by Cambridge University Press

*All material for the manufacture of this book
was sourced from sustainable forests*

CONTENTS

NOTES ON THE MAPS

I have tried to make the maps both clear and uncomplicated. Only two types of line are used – a dotted one to represent lines that have closed to passenger traffic and a solid one for those lines that have always carried passenger trains. To aid identifying stations, each chapter has its own map, which along with the overall county map on pages 6–7 should enable readers to locate the various areas. All maps have north at the top. Restored lines are shown as closed but are given coverage in the relevant chapter.

ABBREVIATIONS

The following abbreviations are used in this book:

B&E	Bristol & Exeter Railway
BR	British Rail (British Railways prior to 1965)
DMU	Diesel multiple unit
GWR	Great Western Railway
LMS	London, Midland & Scottish Railway
LSWR	London & South Western Railway
MR	Midland Railway
S&D	Somerset & Dorset (general reference)
S&DJR	Somerset & Dorset Joint Railway
SR	Southern Railway
WCPR	Weston, Clevedon & Portishead Railway
WSMR	West Somerset Mineral Railway

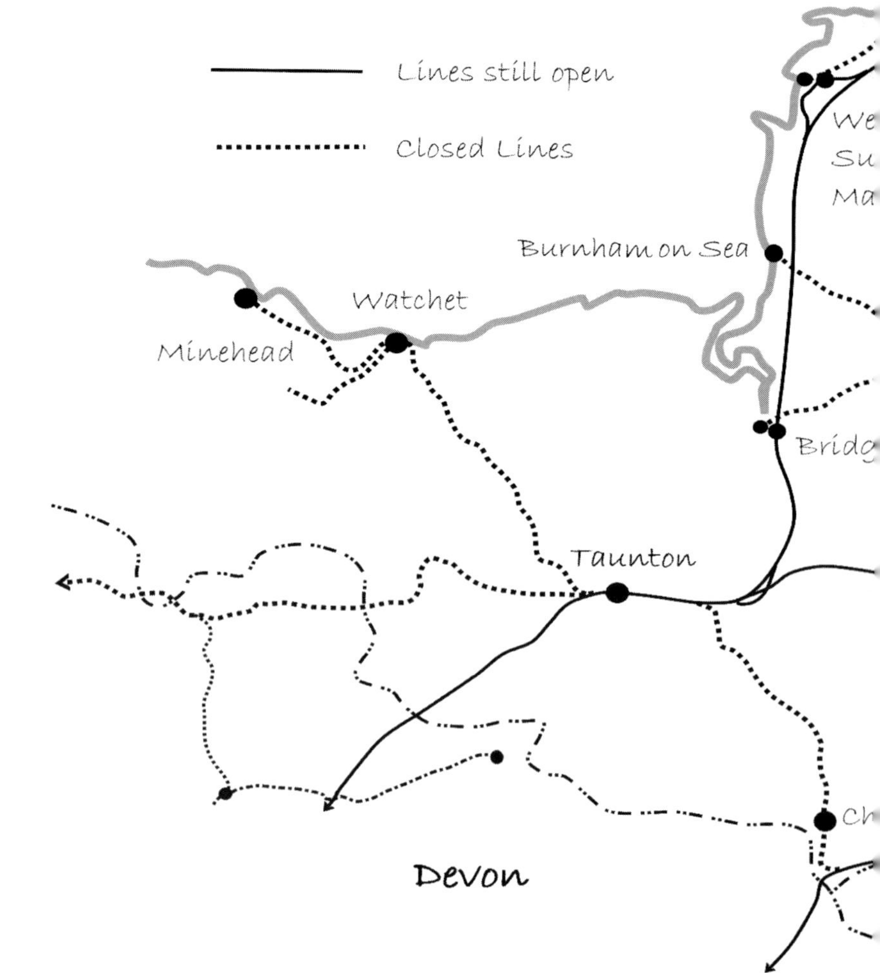

Railways of
Somerset
Lines still open
Closed Lines
We
Su
Ma
Burnham on Sea
Watchet
Minehead
Bridg
Taunton
Devon
Ch

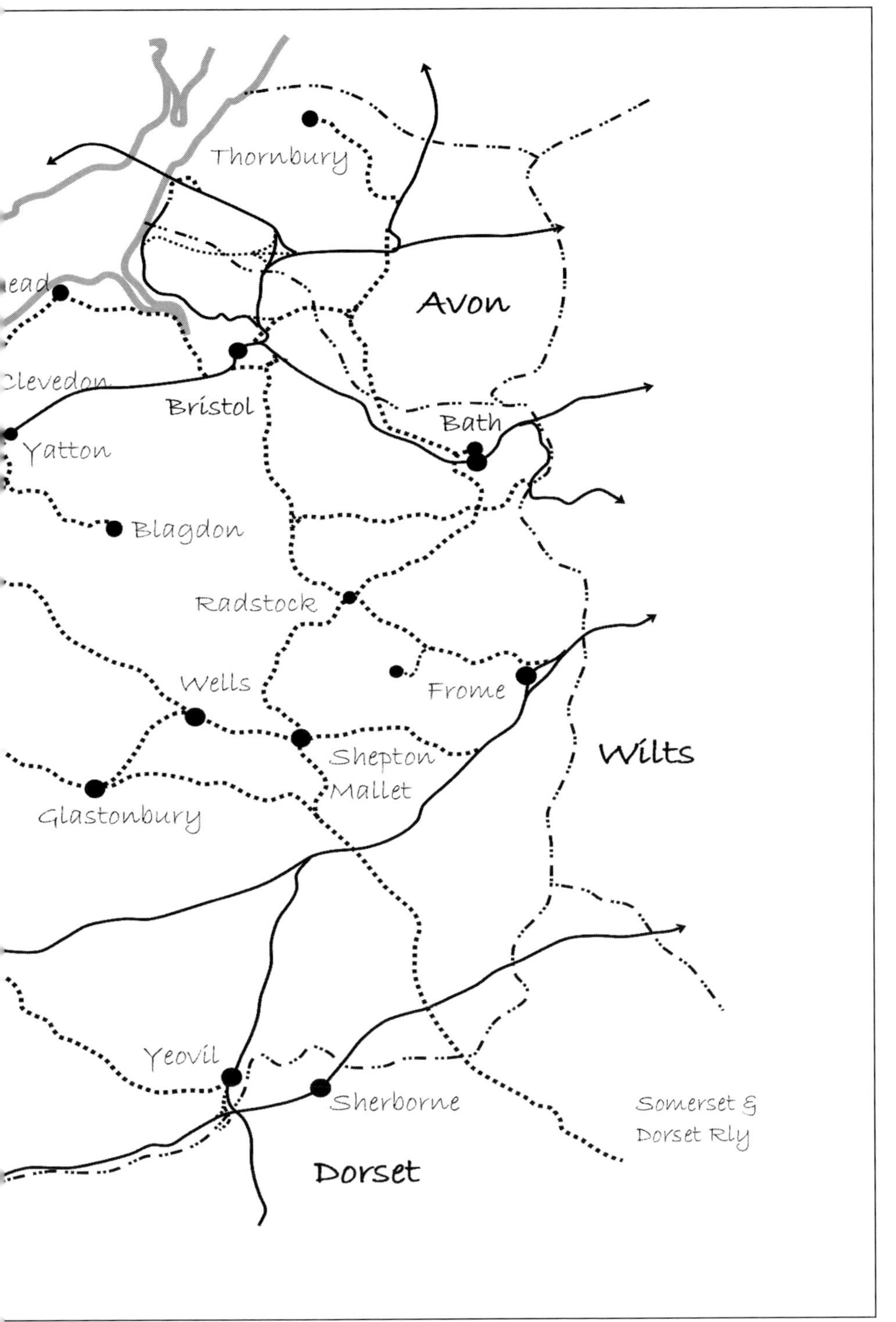

Thornbury
Avon
ead
Clevedon
Bristol
Bath
Yatton
Blagdon
Radstock
Wells
Frome
Wilts
Shepton
Mallet
Glastonbury
Yeovil
Sherborne
Somerset &
Dorset Rly
Dorset

Introduction

How time flies! Writing this book in the early 21st century and looking back to the 1950 to 1960 period, when so much of our old railway system closed, it comes as a shock to realise that most people under the age of 50 will have no first-hand experience of the age of the steam railway. Today, the fact that Somerset had some 400 route miles of railways, of which about 100 still exist, will surprise many. Add to that a once busy coal mining area and a scheme to link South Wales to the English Channel and we can sense that there is more here than one might at first think. This last scheme gave rise to the Somerset & Dorset Joint Railway which became one of the best loved lines in the country, at least by railway enthusiasts.

Somerset is unusual in having had almost all its lines run by the Bristol & Exeter company which in turn was absorbed by the Great Western Railway in 1876. Most rural lines in the West Country were proposed and built by local interests who fought through the red tape of getting their Act through Parliament. The actual running of these lines was undertaken by the 'local' main line company who would take around 50% of the receipts. Usually within a decade or two the main line company would purchase the local one and the line would become simply a part of a larger empire, in our case the GWR.

The London & South Western Railway (LSWR), later to become part of the Southern Railway, ran along the southern edge of Somerset and was to become involved in two short local lines, to Chard and to Yeovil. Meanwhile the Midland Railway had ventured into Bristol from the north and it too was to become involved in the area. This time though it joined the LSWR to acquire and run the Somerset and Dorset line – the only real 'foreign' intrusion into an otherwise GWR-dominated area.

Both the LSWR and the Midland were standard gauge lines, that is the rails were spaced at 4 ft 8½ ins, unlike the Bristol &

Exeter and GWR companies who had adopted Brunel's broad gauge of 7 ft 0¼ in. In the very early days, the standard gauge was often referred to as 'narrow' (particularly by broad gauge men) whereas, since the 1900s, 'narrow' always refers to gauges smaller than the standard.

To read through the history of these lines might make little sense until we make an enormous step – to imagine life without the car and the lorry! Throughout the 19th century, people and goods either moved by horse and cart or by rail. There was very little canal development in the West Country though coastal shipping was important. This dependence on rail for journeys over a few miles long, or for heavy goods like coal, meant that the railway station was a vital addition to a village or town and it is difficult to think of any modest sized town today which didn't have a rail link to aid its growth. Right up to the 1950s, rail travel was the norm for most people, and in particular for holiday travel for the less well off. Summer rail services reached their zenith in this period, far outstripping the glamour of the pre-war expresses.

In this book, I have put the closed lines in geographical groups, and then looked at the history, the route and the traffic of each line in turn. Photographs of many of the stations, along with the trains of yesteryear, will I hope provide at least a feel for this busy past era. Where possible I have included shots of the sites as they are today, but this is becoming very difficult as more and more of the old lines and buildings disappear beneath modern developments and the plough.

Today, in Somerset, we have one major restored line operating steam trains, plus several smaller sites where the sound of steam working still echoes through the air. These restored lines plus the many tracks that can be walked are included in the text.

Stan Yorke

1
Lines Around Taunton

Taunton to Barnstaple
Taunton to Minehead
West Somerset Mineral Railway
Taunton to Chard

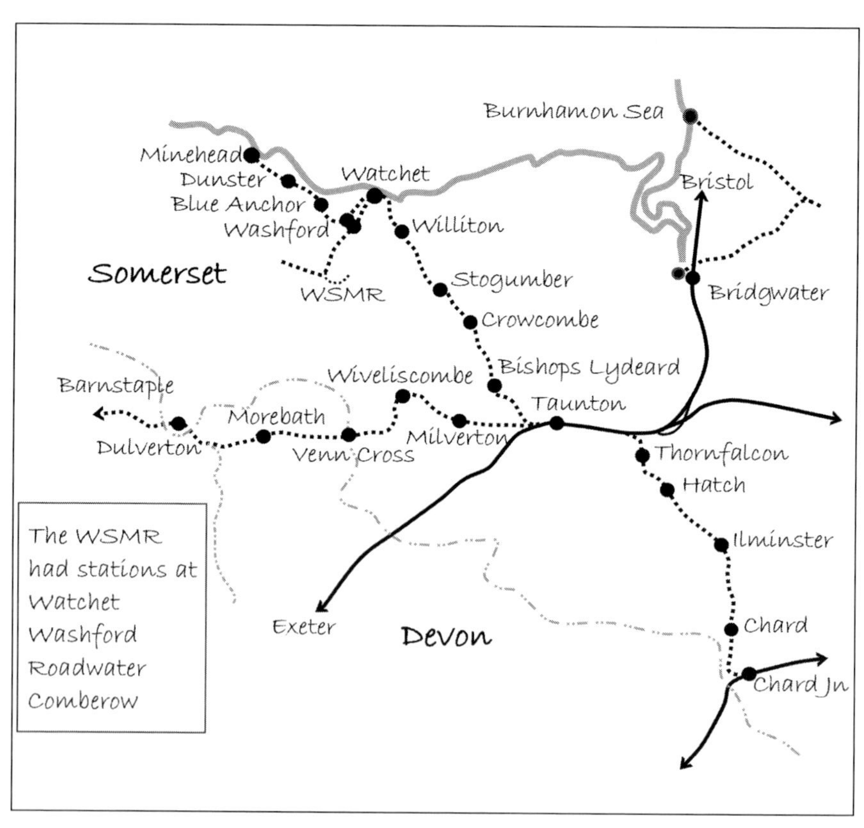

Taunton to Barnstaple

This was a rather unfortunate line in that its totally rural nature was never going to pay the costs of 43 miles of track and 12 signal boxes and stations. The line is covered fully in *Lost Railways of Devon* but as its first 12 miles lie in Somerset it deserves a mention here. The broad gauge line was proposed by the Devon & Somerset Railway Company in 1864, and following various financial difficulties it was opened as far as Wiveliscombe in 1871 and fully opened to Barnstaple by 1873. It left the Bristol & Exeter main line near Norton Fitzwarren, using the same junction as the Minehead branch, and like that line was operated by the Bristol & Exeter from the start.

The service was poor from the word go – mails weren't carried due to a disagreement over the rates, coal was prohibited on the line from Barnstaple because the B&E wanted that to come from Bridgwater via Taunton. Following conversion to standard gauge in 1881 and the link to the LSWR at Barnstaple, the services did improve including through holiday trains to Ilfracombe. There were five trains scheduled on weekdays but there were many

Norton Fitzwarren's enormous signal box which, following the 1937 rebuilding, controlled the four main line tracks and both the Taunton and Minehead junctions. (P.J. Garland)

Milverton was the first station, shown here around 1962, now alas buried under the village bypass. (Lens of Sutton Association)

Wiveliscombe, once the line's terminus, showing the wide track spacing due to the broad gauge berth. (Kidderminster Railway Museum)

sections of low speed around stations and across the viaducts, resulting in an average speed of just 23 miles per hour. In 1901 when the line was absorbed by the GWR, the company already had debts of half a million pounds, an enormous sum in those days. Minor improvements were made and the service rose to eight trains by 1910 plus a couple of goods trains. Services were slowly reduced and by the late 1940s were running at six trains per day.

The early locomotives were the usual GWR types including Metro 2-4-0 tanks, class 1076 Dean Goods 0-6-0 saddle tanks and later the inevitable pannier tanks which in their various classes operated over all the GWR branches. The Metro tanks had been transferred from the Metropolitan Railway in London following its electrification. By the 1930s, the 4300 class 2-6-0 tender locomotives were in use and they became the mainstay of the passenger services. The two wrought iron lattice girder viaducts limited the weight of the locomotives that could be used, though in the later years Southern Railway N class and BR 2-6-2 tanks were used. It has been suggested that it was the state of these two viaducts that helped put the final nails in the coffin of this useful rural line. Incidentally the train frequency mentioned above does not include the increase that took place every summer, particularly with through coaches for Ilfracombe. In 1964 diesel cars took over the local services with some steam-hauled through trains lasting into 1965.

The route used the normal Exeter main line from Taunton as far as Norton Fitzwarren, where a junction was built for the Minehead line, and immediately after leaving the main line tracks the Barnstaple line branched off the Minehead tracks. In 1873 a station was built for Norton Fitzwarren, the main line being the normal two broad gauge tracks. In the early 1930s, extensive alterations were made in the Taunton area with the main line being widened to four tracks to cope with the increased traffic. In 1937, Norton Fitzwarren station was completely rebuilt with four platforms and the junction redesigned to give separate double track pointwork for the Minehead and Barnstaple lines.

The first station on the Barnstaple line was Milverton, just a quarter of a mile from the village, and as part of the 1937 work

Venn Cross in 1962. This station straddled the Somerset/Devon border and was also the first summit. (R.G. Nelson)

the track to Milverton was doubled. Today the next section disappears beneath the village bypass for about a mile before the line continues west, gently climbing to Wiveliscombe, which for a couple of years had been the terminus of the line. Like Milverton it had a passing loop and was well placed for the village. The line now swings south and continues to climb before turning west again towards Bathealton tunnel. Next comes the first lattice girder viaduct over the river Tone, some 100 ft high and 160 yds long, followed by Venn Cross tunnel and station. Beyond here we enter Devon, except for a short four mile section near Dulverton, where the line pops back into Somerset.

This was one of those cross country lines that was very useful to the village communities it served but which fell between two stools; too long to run as a low cost country branch but too far from the larger towns or industries needed to generate traffic and profit. One must wonder what might have been if real economies had been sought earlier.

Having entered Devon the line revisits Somerset for a few miles, ending at Dulverton station, which is seen here in 2007 being converted into private housing. (Author)

In 1966, however, it all ended, the line having been included for closure in the Beeching report of 1963. Today Wiveliscombe station is buried in the centre of a small industrial estate and only the pillars remain from the viaduct over the river Tone. Venn Cross station is now private with just a single signal standing alone in an adjacent field.

Taunton to Minehead

This is the only line in Somerset to be fully restored to steam working after its original closure, but before revelling in the glorious present let's retell the tale of its history.

The original line was built to Watchet harbour by the West Somerset Railway Company from a junction with the Bristol &

Bishops Lydeard in 1912 with trains passing to and from Taunton. (Lens of Sutton Association)

The same scene today with surprisingly little changed. (Author)

Exeter main line near Norton Fitzwarren. Though authorised in 1857, money problems delayed construction and it opened in 1862. In 1865 an extension to Minehead was authorised by the Minehead Railway Company but lapsed in 1870 only to be revived a year later. It opened in 1874 and like the Watchet line was built in broad gauge. Both lines were worked by the Bristol & Exeter which in 1876 was absorbed by the GWR. In 1882 the line was converted to standard gauge and, though the Minehead company had became part of the GWR in 1897, the West Somerset Railway Company remained independent until 1922. The line was built as a single track with passing loops at some of the stations.

Leaving the junction with the Exeter main line, the route went steadily up to Bishops Lydeard where there was a passing loop, a goods yard and shed. The village is somewhat strung out but was nevertheless well served by branch line standards. From here the line, now single, climbed towards the summit at Crowcombe, mostly at around 1 in 80, and we can travel this route today on the preserved West Somerset Railway. We are now in the traditional branch line mode where stations are named after almost anything in the area. Crowcombe village was some 1½ miles away and Heathfield, the original name for the station, was just a farm. There was a passing loop with two platforms but just one short siding, which had originally extended for 2 miles to a quarry in Triscombe. From here to Watchet is a continuous descent, mostly between 1 in 90 and 1 in 100. The next station is at Stogumber but, just before this, a passing loop was installed in 1934 to increase capacity in the summer months. Stogumber had a single platform and a goods loop that passed through the goods shed, the village being a full mile away. The next stop is Williton; although this was a much larger village it was still nearly a mile from its station. The station had a passing loop with two platforms, a small goods yard and shed. There was also a large water tank plus a footbridge and water columns between the platforms.

Watchet station is unusual in that it only has a single platform, although it was probably the most important station on the route to Minehead. When opened in 1862, as the terminus, it had an engine shed as well as a passing loop from which a siding led to

Crowcombe station around 1912 with track still laid in broad gauge manner using well spaced ties rather than regular sleepers. (Lens of Sutton Association)

Stogumber in 1960, still with its loop to the goods shed and possibly a camping coach. (Lens of Sutton Association)

Williton station, again with old style ties rather than conventional sleepers. Note how the former broad gauge space has been used for water columns. This end of the station was altered in 1906 and 1934. (Lens of Sutton Association)

the goods shed and the harbour sidings. Two small turntables allowed trucks to be run along the eastern pier, the western pier being the province of the West Somerset Mineral Line; all the harbour lines were normally worked by horses. Once the extension to Minehead had opened in 1874 the engine shed vanished, some say it was reused at Minehead. The harbour traffic was varied but coal featured throughout the life of the railway connection until it was removed in 1965.

Our route now takes us onto the Minehead Railway Company's tracks as we head west again. Shortly after leaving Watchet station we pass the siding that fed the paper mills (lifted in 1967), quickly followed by the bridge over the West Somerset Mineral Line. Our direction changes slightly to south-west, now running alongside the mineral line, passing the Kentsford Loop, which was installed in 1934 to help handle the rising traffic, and climbs to Washford station. This had a single platform with a goods-only passing loop, which passed through the goods shed,

Watchet was the terminus for 12 years and despite its relative importance it only ever had a single platform. In glorious sunshine 2-6-0 No 9351 sets off for Minehead in the present day. (Author)

plus a short spur. Though like a passing loop, these goods tracks enabled wagons to be drawn into the goods shed from either direction and were never used for passenger trains to pass. Cattle formed an important traffic for Washford which, though a small village, had a cattle market.

The line now swings through 90 degrees to head north-west and back towards the sea, dropping down the 1 in 65 gradient of Washford bank towards Blue Anchor. This was originally called Bradley Gate, but later changed to Blue Anchor after the name of a pub in the nearest village of Carhampton. It was provided with a passing loop with two platforms and a spur that at one time held a camping coach. Most traffic came from the nearby holiday camp site, which gradually developed into a large static caravan park.

Washford follows the same 'loop through the goods shed' layout as Stogumber and Dunster but the station buildings on the extension were to a different design. (Lens of Sutton Association)

The hard work now over, our line runs almost flat towards Minehead, interrupted by the little Dunster station. Dunster village is around ½ mile away but is a very busy tourist spot. Like Washford there was just a single platform with a goods only passing loop running through the goods shed. Two spurs and a siding handled the goods traffic which included coal and timber. For a short period each year, in the polo season at the nearby Dunster Castle, the yard would house horse wagons, which included a compartment for the groom.

After the little level crossing the track was doubled to Minehead in 1934, running straight as a die to the Minehead terminus. The original station had a main platform with a shorter bay, an engine shed and turntable (first of 37 ft 8 in and later of 45 ft) plus the usual goods sidings and shed. Minehead station was extended to handle the summer traffic, which had swollen Minehead from a small village of some 1,500 souls when the

Blue Anchor station around 1910 before the caravans and holidaymakers arrived. Note the extensive planting. (Lens of Sutton Association)

railway arrived to over 6,000 in the 1930s. New sidings were built that swung away from the station into a separate goods yard with two long sidings.

Passenger services started with a modest four trains on weekdays and five on Saturdays. This soon increased to around the seven trains per day mark, reaching a peak in the 1950s of eleven weekday and fifteen Saturday trains plus six on Sunday. Two goods trains ran on weekdays plus a third which only went as far as Watchet. Locomotives followed the usual pattern with Metro 2-4-0 tanks dominating until the 1920s when the 45xx class 2-6-2 tanks joined the fray. Various 0-6-0 tanks were used, with the pannier tanks working right through to the 1960s. DMUs appeared in 1962 along with standard 2-6-2 tanks and type 2 diesels.

In the 1960s freight traffic was concentrated at Taunton and the branch carried on with only passengers. Though the Butlin's camp at Minehead helped, the effect of cars was being felt, as with all branches, and despite economies the line closed in 1971.

Dunster, looking back towards Taunton – probably in the late 1950s. (Lens of Sutton Association)

Preservation

Following a difficult start the West Somerset Railway reopened the Minehead to Blue Anchor section of the line in 1976 as a preserved steam railway. Stogumber was reached in 1978 and finally Bishops Lydeard in 1979. It would obviously have been ideal to have been able to reach Taunton but an almost farcical series of problems followed. Firstly, the National Union of Railwaymen opposed it since their members also drove the local bus service to Taunton. Then in 1983 the now rusting track near Taunton station became part of a siding used by the Taunton Cider Company, who were promptly blamed by BR for preventing the preserved railway from reaching Taunton. This somewhat lame excuse was undermined when the Cider Company stated that they saw no reason why at least some of the steam trains couldn't run past their site and into Taunton. BR then took up the siding and built signals on it for the main line, thus leaving the preserved trains no alternative but to use the main line itself, for which BR wanted a third of a million pounds to

Minehead station in the 1960s, with the goods lines still in use. (Lens of Sutton Association)

The scene today with the goods shed now used for restoration work. The lovingly restored station and trains are probably busier than at any time in the past. (Author)

construct the necessary pointwork and signals. The old bay platform at Taunton, which could have been used so well, was also dismantled. This attitude was often met in the 1970s and 80s by preserved lines struggling to keep a link to the main rail system. Bearing in mind the potential for extra passengers generated by the preserved railways, BR's approach was hardly helpful but then the history of the railways has always put rivalry before commerce. In 1986, the railway opened a halt at Doniford for holidaymakers. It used parts from the closed stations at Montacute and at Cove on the Exe Valley line. Today the line is one of the top preserved lines in the country and well worth a visit.

West Somerset Mineral Railway

The Brendon Hills in West Somerset rise through beautiful wooded valleys to well over 1,000 ft in height and atop these hills are the remains of once active iron mines. The Brendon Hills Iron Ore Company was formed in 1853 by a group of Ebbw Vale ironmasters to develop the mining in the area. It was to serve these mines that the West Somerset Mineral Railway was built between 1856 and 1859, connecting them to the harbour at Watchet. In 1857 there was an unfortunate accident near Watchet involving two locomotives, which killed three men and wrote off one of the engines. The line ran as a conventional railway up the valley of the Washford river to Comberow where a ¾ mile long rope-hauled incline was built. Rising at 1 in 4 to the top of the ridge, it served the mines around Brendon Hill plus an extension that ran 3½ miles west along the ridge to further mines at Gupworthy. Originally it had been hoped to reach Heath Poult a further 2 miles on. The building of a proper engine house and the massive 18 ft diameter winding drums had taken three years, finally reaching full capacity in 1860.

The harbour at Watchet received attention, with the west pier being rebuilt and general dredging. This was a minor drama in its own right as the harbour was believed to be the responsibility of

The reopening celebrations at Watchet station in 1907. (Lens of Sutton Association)

The same spot today with various extensions covering the old trackbed. Even the former railway buildings on the left are under threat. (Author)

Washford station after the reopening. Loco No 37 is approaching from the Brendon direction. (Author's Collection)

the Lord of the Manor and was in an unusable state. Failing to make any progress with the manorial lawyers, the Iron Ore Company promoted a bill during the passage of which it was discovered that the harbour was in fact public property and the Lord of the Manor had no rights at all. Eventually the Watchet Harbour Bill was passed and harbour commissioners took over the responsibility.

Stations were built at Washford, Roadwater and Comberow and in 1865 a passenger service was provided, starting with four trains on weekdays. First and second class fares were advertised but it is doubtful if many people used the small upholstered first class compartments. The rest of the four-wheel coaches were hard, but cheaper, third class accommodation. The 6-mile journey took a leisurely 40 or so minutes, the nominal speed used on the line being a gentle 12 mph behind one of the two Sharp and Stuart 0-6-0 tank engines. Though presumably the passengers were mostly mineworkers the figures are amazing – some 13,000 people were carried in 1866 and around 19,000 just six years later. There was a passenger service on the high level section, which was worked by two Neilson built 0-4-0 saddle tanks, but it never boasted anything as formal as a timetable. Halts on the top section were built at Brendon Hill, Luxborough Road and Gupworthy. Passengers were also provided with a truck in which they were allowed to travel up and down the incline but at their own risk – a practice that was probably quite illegal. Soon after opening, the line was leased by the Ebbw Vale Company who used the iron ore, and who in turn became the Ebbw Vale Steel, Iron and Coal Company. The lease was for 55 years at an annual rent of £5,595.

The quays at Watchet were extended to take 500-ton ships in 1861 and for the next 20 or so years the mineral traffic was good and steady, reaching some 45,000 tons a year. In the mid 1870s a recession had hit the iron trades, plus cheap Spanish ore had come on the market and in 1883 the local mines finally collapsed, leaving some 400 miners and their families with no work or income.

The traffic on the lower section through Washford and Comberow continued with just two daily trains but business still declined until it all closed in 1898; the lease, however, was still being paid! In the early 1890s the company had a protracted

Comberow station around 1890 with a good trade in passengers taking place. (Lens of Sutton Association)

The Brendon Incline, again almost certainly after the reopening in 1907. (Author's Collection)

struggle with the Board of Trade over the lack of safety features on the line, a battle that the company finally lost. Suitably modified, the line gained approval in 1894 but the expense of this work hardly helped.

In 1907 another mining boom started and some of the mines around Brendon Hill reopened, the track was cleaned up, and a kiln (costing £2,000) was built in Washford for refining the ore, though the Gupworthy extension stayed closed.

Following a severe storm in 1900 the commissioners were unable to afford repairs and the harbour was taken over by the District Council, who in 1904 built a new jetty in Watchet harbour. For the reopening a former Metropolitan engine (No 37) plus three coaches were purchased, though there appears to be no record of any formal passenger services being run. A two mile long, narrow, 2 ft gauge line was built to the Colton mines east of Raleigh's Cross; these were reached via a new incline, up which ore was hauled from the workings 250 ft lower down in the quaintly named Galloping Bottom. The 2 ft line was worked by two diminutive locomotives – a Kerr Stuart 0-4-0 and a similar Bagnall engine. Again the supply of iron ore proved fickle and by 1910 it all finally stopped. The jetty was auctioned for £70 and the kiln went for just £5.

Two fleeting events occurred after closure. The first was the use of a section of the line between 1911 and 1913 as a demonstration track for a new Australian train safety scheme known as the Angus System. This was vaguely similar to the GWR design, which provided the driver with a warning if he passed a signal at danger and if no response occurred it would apply the brakes. The second event was the use of the trackbed for a narrow gauge line to convey timber from Watchet to the Washford sawmills. Eventually all the track was commandeered in 1917 and scrapped, and even the two winding drums were blown up, leaving the company with no possessions. The directors moved to abandon the undertaking but one refused and even established a rival company, so until 1919 when the lease and its rather handy income ended, two companies enjoyed the fruits of doing nothing at all! Today part of the line can be walked and the route of the incline can still be seen.

Taunton to Chard

Chard is just in Somerset and was linked to Taunton in 1842 by a canal. Proposals to convert the canal into a railway came and went but Chard still hoped to be part of a main line route, preferably over the twelve or so miles to Taunton. The first line in the area, the London & South Western Railway route to Exeter, passed by some 2½ miles to the south and in 1863 a locally funded branch was opened from this line to Chard Town station. Quickly absorbed by the LSWR this branch was standard gauge, as indeed was all of the LSWR. In 1861 powers were obtained by another local company to build a line alongside the canal to Taunton with the company being promptly absorbed by the Bristol & Exeter, which had purchased the old canal and closed it down. This broad gauge line was opened in 1866 and was joined by an extension from the LSWR line originally intended to allow the LSWR to reach the Chard canal basin. The shared station, Chard Joint, had two services of different gauges, which helped to maintain the 'them and us' atmosphere – the two companies kept their own staff and signal boxes. Even the turntable was fitted with both broad and standard gauge track. In 1891 the GWR

Thornfalcon station with its somewhat dangerous approach through the busy goods yard. Taken in 1959. (Lens of Sutton Association)

(formerly Bristol & Exeter) branch was converted to standard gauge, though it took until 1917 for sense to overcome prejudice and the LSWR Town station was closed to passengers, leaving the GWR to work the trains from Taunton through Chard Joint (later Central) and on to Chard Junction on the LSWR line.

The early service on the short LSWR section started with five trains a day and reached twelve in 1914. The GWR Taunton section had seven per day, plus one on Sundays. After 1917, when the GWR took over the running, the through timetable carried on with seven weekday trains and one on Sunday from Chard to Taunton. Even though these were through trains they always stopped in Chard for a long period as though nothing had changed from the two company days – typical childish GWR tactics, I'm afraid.

Trains usually left Taunton from the No 2 bay platform, staying on the main line until Creech junction where the branch turned

Ilminster station with a cheerful but neglected pannier tank setting off for Chard. (R.E. Toop)

Today the station building and the very large goods shed are still in use though all signs of the track have gone. (Author)

south towards Thornfalcon. This station was nearer to Henlade, which was more populated than Thornfalcon, and though not a passing place it had a busy little goods yard through which passengers had to walk to reach the station. Hatch station came next, sensibly near the village of Hatch Beauchamp, and was provided with another neat and busy goods yard. Next was Ilton Halt, opened in 1928, some way from its large village. We now reach Ilminster, the only other town of any real size apart from Chard, provided with a reasonably sized goods yard but again nearly a mile from the town centre. Another small wooden platform halt was built in 1928 to serve Donyatt, a straggling village the other side of the little river Isle.

Chard itself was hardly a large town (population around 6,000) but its stations were around ½ mile from the original town centre. During the 20th century the town expanded towards the railway and one can't help wondering whether, today, a rail link would be viable. It had a turntable, an engine shed and a goods yard. There

Chard station in the 1960s with 5504 and two coaches waiting to set off to the junction. (Lens of Sutton Association)

The same view today with the station buildings in use. Note the bracket and stone column virtually untouched. (Author)

was a bay platform at each end, which allowed the two companies to pretend the other wasn't there, plus the single through platform used after 1917. The original LSWR Town station, some ½ mile south, was operational until 1916 when it became Chard Town Goods and it remained in use as a goods depot to the end. The run to the former LSWR main line at Chard Junction had no intermediate stations, the single line curving into its own bay platform at the junction. Passengers had to cross a road to gain entry to the main station and the London to Exeter line platforms. There was a single siding, which gave a connection between the two lines so that goods could be transferred.

With only Ilminster of any size apart from Chard and no other industrial traffic, it was inevitable that the line would struggle. In 1962 the passenger service ended, followed two years later by the Taunton–Chard goods traffic. A bitumen distribution depot was opened around 1960 in Chard goods yard but it all closed in 1966. It is a shame that Chard, like Yeovil, was situated on a tributary running north to south and not in an east to west valley, when the LSWR might well have served the town directly.

Chard Junction with the rather lonely branch platform and a pannier loco and coaches. (Author's Collection)

2
The Somerset &
Dorset Railway

The Slow and Dirty
Branches to Burnham and Bridgwater
The Wells branch
Fame at last – the branch to Bath

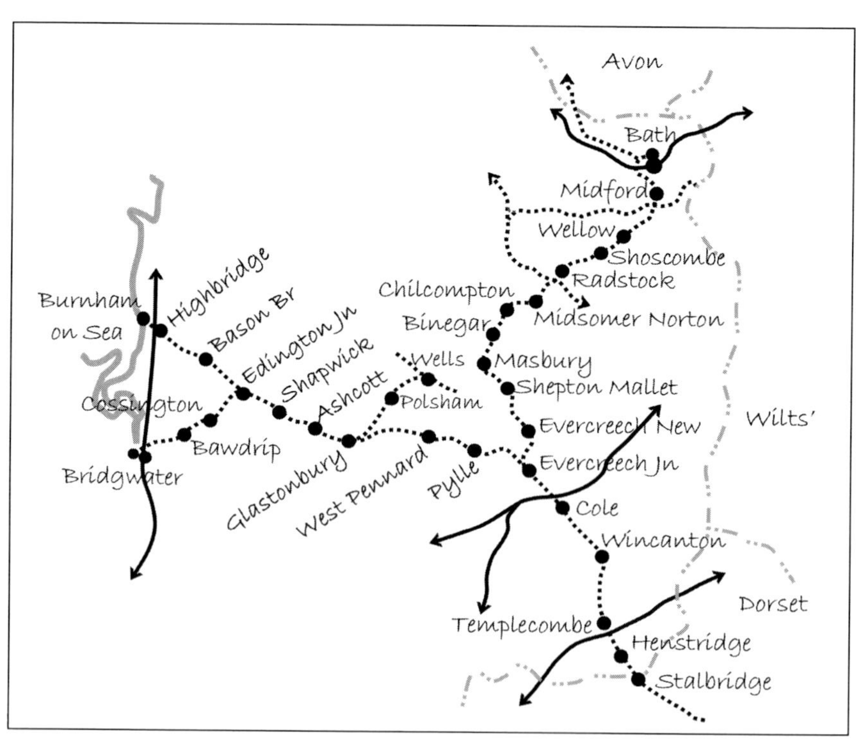

The Slow and Dirty

*'And here, to the rhythm of the Somerset and Dorset
Joint Railway, dream again that ambitious Victorian dream
which caused this long railway still to be running through
deepest, quietist, flattest, remotest, least spoilt Somerset.'*

John Betjeman, 1963

Probably no other line in Britain engenders the nostalgic following generated by the S&D. This is partly due to its dramatic geography and partly to its joint Midland and Southern ownership, which provided a delightful variety of locomotives and coaching stock. Like many long-gone lines, its simple initials invited nicknames. Slow and Dirty was already in use in the 1870s, to be followed by Swift and Delightful and, at the end, by Sabotaged and Defeated. Though the line had various owners and formal titles over the years I have kept to the popular Somerset & Dorset (S&D) which stayed with the line to the end. Its origins are in two quite separate companies. The oldest, the Somerset Central Railway, was born of the drive of the Clark family of Glastonbury who had progressed from being skin dressers and sheepskin rug makers to becoming shoe manufacturers. The Somerset Central built a single track, 12 mile, broad gauge line from Highbridge to Glastonbury in 1854, which was extended south to Cole in 1862. The line joined the Bristol & Exeter main line at Highbridge and indeed the B&E operated the line from the start. Two extensions were quickly added – to Burnham, just 1½ miles from Highbridge, and to Wells, 6 miles on from Glastonbury, both opened by 1859. Wells had hoped to find itself on a more important through route but history was to deal it quantity rather than quality, as we will see. The second company was the Dorset Central Railway, which had opened a standard gauge line from Wimborne to Blandford in 1860. The two companies, seeing that their intended lines would complete a useful north–south link, joined forces as the Somerset & Dorset Railway in 1862.

In 1862 the broad gauge line was further extended to Templecombe where the LSWR crossed on its way to Exeter, and just a year later it reached Blandford. Inspired by hopes of traffic from South Wales to the southern coast of England the company purchased steam ships to operate between Cardiff and Highbridge, but the venture was not well founded and cost the company money it could ill afford. By now the broad gauge line had laid a third rail enabling standard gauge trains to run throughout. The new company, now responsible for running its own line, had inherited dreadful debts and in 1866 it was put into receivership. Four difficult years followed but by 1870 the receiver was discharged and the company could continue its insatiable desire for expansion. Running mixed gauge stock was always going to be a pain and in 1870 the S&D rid itself of the broad gauge track and became a standard gauge line throughout.

The next fling was the extension to Bath to join the Midland Railway. First mooted in 1870, work started in 1872 and was

A very early S&D loco, predating the 'Joint' company so probably around the 1860s. Though from a London company the loco may well have been assembled in the Highbridge works. (Brunel University/Clinker Collection)

complete by 1874 – in view of the engineering this was quite an achievement. It was this line that was to completely change the S&D, for not only did it pass through the Somerset coalfields but it linked the system to the Midlands without using the Bristol & Exeter's lines. By 1876, faced with near bankruptcy again and following more intrigue with the GWR and the Bristol & Exeter, the S&D leased its line to the Midland Railway and the LSWR for 999 years becoming the Somerset & Dorset Joint Railway. Though not in Somerset, the same year saw the route of the southern end changed from Wimborne to Broadstone and thus into Bournemouth. The Templecombe to Blandford section was only single track as was the Highbridge line to Evercreech, reflecting the original rural nature of the system. In 1923, the wartime (1914–18) arrangement for operating the rail system as a united industry, free from local competition, was given formal status in the so called grouping. The S&D became vested jointly between the Southern Railway and the London, Midland and Scottish Railway.

The original section to Highbridge survived until 1966 when the entire S&D system was closed.

Branches to Burnham and Bridgwater

The short extension from Highbridge to Burnham on Sea involved crossing the Bristol & Exeter line on the level after which it passed the siding to the local wharf on the river Brue and, gently climbing, entered Burnham. Beyond the station there was a long stone causeway at which ships could dock. Unfortunately this section of the track dropped at 1 in 23 onto the causeway and it was deemed too dangerous for locomotives, so passengers had to walk to and from the boats to the station. Goods wagons were hauled up and down the slope by cables. Despite several attempts the harbour at Burnham was not to prosper. Silting and the wind-blown, open nature of the terrain did not bode well and railway owned shipping finished in 1888. Highbridge wharf, however, did better and enjoyed a steadily increasing trade well into the

1930s. A locomotive and carriage works was also sited at Highbridge. Almost completely rebuilt and expanded in the 1870s, it served the line until its closure in 1930 when the locomotive stock became entirely handled by the LMS. Around 300 men lost their jobs, some families moving to Derby or Swindon to stay in railway work. The Highbridge works was a remarkable feature involved in building much of the coaching stock and carrying out maintenance on the wide range of locomotives. It was here that the Prussian blue paintwork had been introduced, making S&D trains a most impressive sight. After 1930 locos were painted in plain black and the coaching stock became the normal Southern Railway green.

In 1951 the passenger service from Highbridge to Burnham ended with excursion traffic limping on until 1962.

The idea of a branch to Bridgwater from the Glastonbury area had come up several times; it had been the preferred destination back in the 1850s but crossing the intervening hills had been seen as an expense too far. The Bridgwater branch was eventually built in 1890, following years of high jinks by the Bristol & Exeter

Wincanton, on the original route to join the Dorset Central line. (Kidderminster Railway Museum)

Pylle station on the first extension to Cole in 1862. Seen here in 1956. (Kidderminster Railway Museum)

Glastonbury, possibly the true home of the S&D. In later years the Wells branch left from the far left platform and ran out towards Polsham independently of the route to Pylle. (Kidderminster Railway Museum)

Ashcott station, as the line to Burnham set out across the low, flat land of the Somerset Marshes. (Brunel University/Mowat Collection)

Bason Bridge in 1933 with the flat land characteristic of the area plain to see. (Brunel University/Mowat Collection)

Highbridge where the S&D crossed over the GWR main line en route to Burnham. The station was immediately behind the camera. (Author's Collection)

Today even though the road bridge is the same there is no trace of the crossing. The old S&D station has disappeared beneath modern apartment blocks, including the signal box. (Author)

company in its attempts to defend its patch, which of course included Highbridge and Bridgwater. It defeated an earlier S&D proposal to reach Bridgwater by adding a third rail to the broad gauge main line from Highbridge and Bridgwater and then from Cogload junction and east to the branch to Yeovil. It even ran a standard gauge passenger service from Yeovil to Bridgwater and Highbridge, where there was a connection to the Somerset & Dorset, in a desperate attempt to show that there was no need for an S&D line to Bridgwater. The Bristol & Exeter company and the GWR did everything they could to discourage the tradesmen of Bridgwater from sending goods onto the S&D lines via Highbridge. The Bristol & Exeter had good cause to defend its business as Bridgwater was a very prosperous town; its docks, now well served by rail, handled large quantities of coal, much of which was then distributed by rail, and the local brick making works generated yet more rail traffic. In 1874 it had reached some 200,000 tons of rail-borne goods, aided no doubt by the Bridgwater to Taunton canal whose basin formed part of the harbour facilities in Bridgwater.

Burnham, complete with long storage sidings for holiday trains. Behind the camera the line went on to the little pier. Taken in 1933. (Brunel University/Mowat Collection)

The Bridgwater branch needed a junction on the Burnham line and it was here at Edington. The branch track can just be seen in the distance veering to the left in 1949. (Kidderminster Railway Museum)

In 1875 another bill for the branch was defeated, this time by straightforward bribery and corruption though it took some years for the whole story to emerge. Though the merchants of Bridgwater had complained endlessly at the B&E monopoly, when it came to investing real money in an alternative company they were nowhere to be seen! By 1876 the Somerset & Dorset Railway had been taken over by the joint LSWR and Midland Railway companies and the Bristol & Exeter had been absorbed by the GWR. Following more campaigning, yet another Bridgwater Railway Bill was proposed and this time passed. The new line, opened in 1890, had been built by the Bridgwater Railway Company and was operated by the Somerset & Dorset Joint Railway – and was to all intents and purposes a branch of the S&DJR.

The single line set out from Edington Junction, on the Highbridge section, and its 7 mile journey was punctuated by a station at Cossington and later a halt at Bawdrip. In Bridgwater it crossed over the GWR main line to reach its own terminus adjacent to Bristol Road. There was a goods yard, engine shed and turntable and from the furthest siding a branch set off via a large curve to a wharf alongside the river Parrett. This siding would later feed a cement, lime and brick works. Another cement works was also served via a spur, which left the line just before the station was reached.

Initially the service was good, even including two express runs from Bridgwater to Templecombe where connections were made with LSWR trains to London. Some nine trains ran daily with a goods service to and from Templecombe. By 1914, however, this had reduced to six trains and the 'express' service had ceased. The normal train consisted of three or four six-wheeled coaches pulled by a Johnson 0-4-4 tank locomotive, although sometimes an S&D 0-6-0 tank would be used. In the late 1920s push-pull auto working was introduced both to the Bridgwater trains and to the Wells and Burnham services. This seems to have lasted up to the war after which conventional trains ran, still using the Johnson tanks or LMS 0-6-0 tanks. After the war there was still a service of five or six trains but by 1952 this had been reduced to only four very poorly used trains. Closure was inevitable, though goods traffic lasted for two more years, until 1954.

The line had been born of complaints rather than a clearly identified need, and it had never made any profit. Indeed it had opened so late in the railway era that it faced competition from improved roads before it had even reached its 20th birthday.

The Wells branch

The first proposals by the Somerset Central Railway were for a line from Highbridge to Wells, and then to proceed towards Frome. In the event the main line went south from Glastonbury and headed towards Blandford in order to meet the Dorset Central line. This displeased some of the shareholders from Wells, who protested and instead got a branch to their city as second best. The branch opened in 1859 and for three years was the end

The only stop on the Wells branch was at Polsham, seen here in 1949 just two years before closure. (Kidderminster Railway Museum)

of the line from Highbridge. In 1862 the 'main' line was constructed, leaving the Wells line at the Wells branch junction. In 1878 the junction was closed and a second line added to take the Wells line back into Glastonbury station independently of the main line, which headed south. It was built in broad gauge, but like the other sections received a third standard gauge rail in 1864, with the broad gauge being abandoned completely in 1870.

There was just one intermediate station, at Polsham, though the entire area is somewhat devoid of population. In Wells the S&D station was named Priory Road and comprised a station with a single, rather dreary platform, an engine shed and a quaint waterwheel-driven water pump which fed the water tower.

Two other companies now enter the story. One was the East Somerset Railway, which built its broad gauge line from Witham to Shepton Mallet in 1858 (see Chapter 4) and then extended it to Wells in 1862. The other was the Cheddar Valley & Yatton

Railway, which opened its broad gauge line from Yatton, on the Bristol & Exeter main line, to Cheddar in 1869 and continued to Wells Tucker Street by 1870. We now have three stations in Wells – two broad gauge termini separated by a standard gauge terminus. The S&D agreed to allow the two broad gauge lines to join via a line through their property, but the Board of Trade objected on safety grounds. Eventually, by 1875 both of these lines had converted to standard gauge and all three stations were joined.

The S&D branch was worked as a single block from Glastonbury to Wells. Initially there were seven trains a day from Highbridge to Wells plus two on Sundays. This dropped to six with no Sunday service as the company went through its desperate early years. In 1874 when the extension to Bath opened, the services in general improved and by the early 1900s Wells had ten trains a day. Two goods trains ran in the 1930s. The service, however, dropped slowly until after the war there was one goods train a day and a very spartan passenger service.

The S&D continued to use its Priory Road station until it closed to traffic in 1951. During the last few years an average of just six passengers a day had used the line!

Fame at last – the branch to Bath

Following the end of the broad gauge track in 1870 the S&D obtained an Act for a line from Evercreech to Bath in 1871, and just three years later the line was open. Strictly speaking the S&D line ends at Bath Junction where it joined the existing Midland line to Bath Green Park (Queen Square). This line contained almost all the difficult engineering as it climbed across the Mendip Hills, visiting Shepton Mallet and Radstock on the way. There are so many steep sections that it is easier to comment on the level bits! Except for the 5 miles between Midford and Radstock the rest of the 25 mile section is dominated by gradients between 1 in 50 and 1 in 100, the summit of 811 ft being reached just before Masbury. Nearly a mile and a half of tunnels plus

Shepton Mallet (Carlton Road) looking south in 1949. The station was not well placed for the town and is now a large factory estate. (Kidderminster Railway Museum)

seven large viaducts were needed. Incidentally Combe Down tunnel, just 2½ miles from Bath, was a single bore and the longest tunnel in Britain built without ventilation shafts – a mile of very hot and smoky driving. The other surprise is that Radstock was the centre of the Somerset coal mining area, an industrial blot on an otherwise rural journey. It was this vital link to the Midlands that gave the S&D a real function, without which it was just a useful rural line to link a selection of small towns in an area dominated by wool and later agriculture. Like much of the original S&D, the line from Bath was built with just a single track.

Within a month of the Midland and LSWR leasing the line a serious accident, caused by negligence, occurred near Radstock. This resulted in the death of 13 people and injury to a further 34, and brought unwanted publicity to the S&D. On the night of the August Bank Holiday two crowded trains, one from the Bath Regatta and one heading north from Wimborne, ploughed into

Masbury station in 1937 showing a hard working ex-Midland 4-4-0 with at least six coaches having just crossed the summit. (H.C. Casserley)

Masbury station today, now a private residence. The station and platforms are still clearly intact. (Author)

each other on a single section of track. The noise was heard five miles away and the sound of engine whistles and escaping steam, mingled with the cries of the injured, must have been terrible. The enquiry revealed poorly trained staff and the haphazard way the line was operated – problems that the new owners tackled with commendable speed and enthusiasm. Two further mishaps occurred in later years on the steep run down to Bath. In 1929 a goods train ran out of control on the precipitous 1½ mile section to Bath Junction, and in 1936 an unmanned engine repeated the terrifying journey before becoming derailed.

The new owners of what was now named the Somerset & Dorset Joint Railway carried out the doubling of the track wherever possible. By 1905, only 26 miles of single track were left

Binegar in 1965. The northbound crews could relax a little with the line mostly downhill, though those going south were now exhausted. (Kidderminster Railway Museum)

Chilcompton station on one of the double track sections built in the 1880s. (Author's Collection)

of the 64 miles of the Bath–Bournemouth route. The single sections, though, still caused delays as the locomotives had to slow down to 10 mph (4 mph at night) in order to exchange the tokens by hand. It was to alleviate this that Alfred Whitaker, the Highbridge loco works superintendent, invented his automatic tablet-exchanging apparatus. Tested out on the Bridgwater branch this was installed on the main line in 1904, greatly reducing the delays as the locomotives could now exchange tokens at a much higher speed.

The link to the Midland line at Bath enabled holiday trains from the Midlands and further north to gain access to the resorts around Bournemouth, and it was these heavily-used summer Saturday trains that form the core of the romantic memories of the Somerset & Dorset line.

Around 1900 the company introduced its new livery, when engines and coaches were painted in Prussian Blue with gold

Midsomer Norton station in 1961. The line (although high above the town) was fairly close. (Kidderminster Railway Museum)

Today the site is the home of the Somerset & Dorset Railway, which is slowly reopening a section of the old line. (Author)

Radstock goods depot in 1928 with an LMS 4-4-0 drawing its train towards the station. (Author's Collection)

lines. Company crests adorned the coach sides and the locomotives carried their number on a bright red buffer beam.

The passenger service started with around four weekday trains, which ran through to Bournemouth including two that carried through coaches from Birmingham. In the first year over 100,000 tons of goods were transferred to the Midland Railway in Bath, plus nearly 90,000 tons to the LSWR at Templecombe. Traffic steadily increased throughout the 1900s but, as everywhere else, the motor car and lorry were eating into the traffic.

All manner of locomotives were used on the hilly section from Bath to Evercreech, including Johnson 4-4-0s which could handle four-coach trains on their own. In 1914 eleven Fowler-designed 2-8-0 engines were supplied, which performed sterling work on the heavy trains. The 1920s saw the arrival of five 0-6-0 class 4

Wellow station was built, like many on the Bath extension, in grey limestone and slate. This was a well patronised stop as the village only had a bus service once a week! (Author's Collection)

Midford station was the start of the final single line section into Bath. The signalman here had to be on his toes on busy summer Saturdays when any delay could cause chaos further south. A replica of this box can be seen in the S&D museum at Williton on the Minehead line. (Kidderminster Railway Museum)

freight locomotives and more LMS class 2 passenger locomotives, which were to become the workhorses of the line until closure. In the late 1930s, following strengthening of the bridges on the Avon valley line to Bath, which all LMS locos had to use, the Stanier 'Black Fives' arrived. Without doubt one of the best engines ever produced, these took the S&D in their stride and, along with their BR derivatives, formed the backbone of the heavy services until the end.

After 1950 the SR Bullied Pacifics were tried on the heavy holiday traffic trains, but still needed the help of a second locomotive for trains of more than eight coaches. They were something of a disappointment and were only used for a few years. Finally the class 9 BR 2-10-0s were used, which could take the heaviest trains on their own. Though a wonderful sight these large engines consumed vast quantities of water and coal. When going flat out up the steep sections the injectors would be

The end of the journey, at least for the engine and crew, Bath Green Park station. The delightful structure still proudly stands though now it functions as part of Sainsbury's car park. (Author)

continuously running to keep the boiler filled with water. The fireman would also be working flat out putting nearly a hundredweight of coal onto the fire every minute!

Though not obvious to the traveller the two long gradients – Radstock to Masbury and Evercreech to Masbury, both around 8 miles long – demanded an extraordinary performance from the engines and the crew. It was the duration of these climbs, mostly at around 1 in 50, that caused all sorts of problems. Goods engines that could make the climb failed when it came to slowing a long train of loose-coupled wagons, due to inadequate brakes. Locomotives that could produce a brave dash of power became winded when faced with the need to raise large quantities of steam for 20 minutes or more. The ride was also tortuous with dozens of mini summits for the driver to cope with.

Just how busy the line became in the 1950s almost defies belief, when we remember that the route included several single track sections. The technique was to group the long distance holiday trains – northbound in the morning and southbound in the afternoon.

For instance in a period of just over one hour in the morning, separate trains ran through the S&D bound for Liverpool, Manchester, Leeds, Bradford, Cleethorpes and Derby. These were usually long trains needing two locomotives to climb over the Mendip Hills. The afternoons became more difficult as, although the bulk of through trains ran south, there were still relief trains going north. At Midford, at the end of the single line from Bath, on a typical August Saturday six long distance trains passed each other in 40 minutes – a train from Cleethorpes passed one going back to Birmingham. From Sheffield a train passed one to Coventry, and one from Bradford passed a train going north to Walsall. Again many of these were double headed and desperately trying to keep to time in order to vacate a single section and allow another train to enter it without delay.

Throughout the life of the S&D freight traffic was very important. In the early 1900s it provided more revenue than passengers and accounted for a lot of trains. Around 20 goods trains ran over the Bath–Templecombe section every day, both ways. Most of these ran at night to ease the daytime congestion.

With this very brief description of the traffic levels it is easy to see why the trains attracted such attention from fans of railways. At times virtually every engine that could move was commandeered, providing an ever changing and interesting succession of locomotives working hard over the heavily graded line.

By 1930, a reorganisation was deemed necessary with the LMS looking after the trains and the SR looking after the track and civil engineering matters. Though local traffic declined, the through holiday traffic increased. During the Second World War the strategic importance of the line saw intense use for moving troops and equipment to the south coast. After the war, with petrol still rationed, passenger traffic stayed buoyant. But following the formation of British Railways in 1947, we see a tragic series of events so typical of the mismanagement of the 1950s and 60s. The line was, of course, partly in the traditional GWR area and following endless boundary changes the former GWR men had their revenge on this impudent intruder. Everything that could be done to discourage traffic was done and by 1966 closure was complete.

Today the not inconsiderable towns of Wells, Glastonbury, Radstock and Shepton Mallet have no rail links at all and the open marshes now echo to the M5 rather than the friendly clank of an old loco pulling a few coaches to Highbridge or Bridgwater. The Mendip Hills have returned to peace once more with the thundering sounds of heavy trains long gone. Rest in peace, you hard-working friend of so many Somerset towns and villages.

3
Yeovil

How not to do it!
The Taunton to Yeovil branch

Somerset
Bristol
Westbury
Athelney
Durston
London
Taunton
Langport
West
Thorney & Kingsbury
Martock
Yeovil
Montacute
Hendford
Sherborne
Dorset
Chard
Devon
Exeter
Hendford
Halt
Yeovil
Pen Mill
Hendford
Goods
Yeovil
Town
(Joint)
Wartime Link
Yeovil Junction

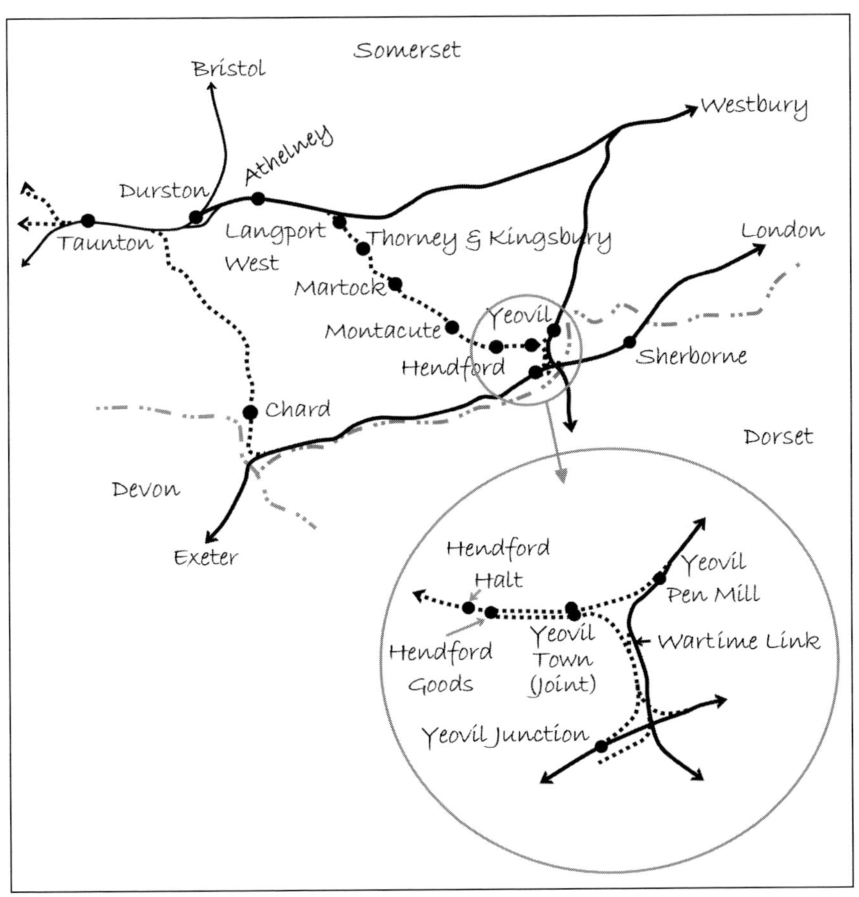

How not to do it!

Yeovil was a very old town, famed for its tanning, leather dressing and glove making activities as well as its thriving flax and linen industry. It was also a centre for the coaching routes of the region and was on the post route to Devon and Cornwall. Though the linen industry had shrunk by the 1840s it was still a lively and industrious area. The first railway to approach Yeovil came from Taunton, being opened to Hendford on the town's western outskirts in 1853. The arrival of the first train was greeted with great celebrations – the good and noble came to meet the Bristol & Exeter directors, the shops closed and the local band played throughout. It is very hard for us to imagine just how important the railways were in the 1800s both to commerce and the general public.

Built by the Bristol & Exeter in broad gauge with a third rail added later for standard gauge traffic, it was extended in 1856 to join the GWR backed Wilts, Somerset & Weymouth line which had just reached Yeovil Pen Mill station. This line had its own bewildering history and the section through Yeovil was built virtually as a loss making line to curtail the LSWR's ambitions in what Paddington (GWR headquarters) saw as their territory. Most of this line is still open so I will merely identify it as the line from Castle Cary to Weymouth via Yeovil.

In 1860 the Salisbury & Yeovil Railway (all but owned by the LSWR) had reached Yeovil by means of a short diversion from its intended line to Exeter, again using Hendford station.

Within a year the slightly more useful joint (LSWR and Bristol & Exeter) Town station was opened and Hendford became just a goods depot. There were now three companies in Yeovil – the Bristol & Exeter from Taunton, the LSWR from Salisbury and the GWR from Frome, via Castle Cary – all rivals and slightly suspicious of each other.

The LSWR didn't envisage a through service to Yeovil from its main line and as soon as this line moved on towards Exeter, it built Yeovil Junction station on the Exeter line to serve the short branch to Yeovil. Rather than build the junction where the original

Yeovil Junction and on the right the remains of the Clifton Maybank exchange shed. Along with the turntable, this area is now used by the Yeovil Railway Centre. (Author)

curve left for Yeovil it chose a spot further west involving a new, west facing curve – one might have thought that a LSWR stopping service heading for Exeter would have been able to run over the old curve into Yeovil, reverse and, using the new west facing curve, continue its journey, thus providing the town with a through rail link. Instead the original eastern curve was abandoned. As the Town station was all the LSWR needed for a simple shuttle service to and from the junction, its line to Hendford became just a long goods siding.

The joint station was originally little more than two stations sitting nervously together; each had its own east and west signal box, station master's house, booking office and station staff, plus a 'joint' staff who presumably kept the other staff from fighting! The signal boxes were replaced by just two in 1902, which in turn were replaced by one 55 lever box in 1916.

Yeovil Pen Mill station in 1963 with a pannier tank ready to haul its train to the town station and on to Taunton. (Kidderminster Railway Museum)

The same spot today with almost everything still in place. The line to the town station is now a footpath but the junction and Weymouth lines are still in use. (Author)

Yet another Yeovil station, known as Clifton Maybank, was opened in 1864 next to the LSWR Junction station, albeit only for the interchange of goods between the two gauges.

A traveller innocently going from, say, Dorchester to Exeter would find that they had to change at Pen Mill and catch a Taunton train for the one mile journey to the Town station, where they would change for the shuttle service down to the Junction station, where they would change yet again for the LSWR main line to Exeter. Despite this chaos all three passenger stations handled useful numbers right up to the early 1950s, and indeed Pen Mill station still provides Yeovil with a rail service.

The effect of the rail connections on the prosperity of the town was instant. Between 1800 and 1860 the population had more than trebled; in 1856 over 400,000 pairs of gloves had been manufactured. Surprisingly, even in the 1950s Yeovil made half of all the gloves produced in England. In the 1880s Messrs Aplin and Barrett started the Western Counties Creamery, which went on to give us the 'St Ivel' brand name. The other company that was to bring much prosperity to the town was Petters, which started as an ironmonger's and soon spread into manufacturing electrical equipment and engines, with diesel engines remaining their core product for many years. In 1913 a new factory was built at Westland – just beyond the Hendford goods depot – and added the wartime manufacture of aircraft to the engine work. In 1935 the aircraft division took over the factory as Westland Aircraft Ltd and in 1948 they gained the manufacturing rights for the Sikorsky helicopters. Today helicopter production has made them the town's largest employer.

I entitled this section 'How not to do it' and maybe the following comments from a local paper in 1860 may show just how indifferent the rail companies were to the lot of their poor customers. 'Neither the Great Western nor the Bristol and Exeter staff had any interest in passengers attempting to use the LSWR trains, or for that matter, the trains of any company except their own. There are no refreshment rooms at Hendford station, the scene of the most intolerable waiting by which the railway system of this district, or perhaps of the whole country, is deformed. Everything seems at present contrived to render travelling by the whole three lines converging at Yeovil positively disagreeable as well as inconvenient.'

The Taunton to Yeovil branch

Built by the Bristol & Exeter company as a broad gauge line, this set out from the western outskirts of Yeovil and reached Martock in 1849, but lay unused due to the usual money problems. These were finally resolved in 1853 and the rest of the route to Durston on the main line to Taunton was opened. This was extended to meet the GWR line from Frome at Yeovil Pen Mill station in 1856.

There is a lovely comment recorded at this time when the town watchmen of Yeovil requested and received an extra shilling on account of the number of navvies in the town.

This could be a good point at which to comment on the engineering of what at first glance seems a simple rural line. The

Yeovil Town station in the 1930s. The right hand platform handled the LSWR/SR trains whilst the GWR line to Taunton used the left hand side. Today it is all under a retail park. (Brunel University/Mowat Collection)

Hendford Halt opened in 1932 to serve the increasing industry in the area. The original station and the goods yard are behind the camera. (Lens of Sutton Association)

Montacute station in 1964 with a class 3 BR 2-6-2 tank engine and train en route to Yeovil. The whole of this end of the line has disappeared beneath a new road. (Lens of Sutton Association)

Martock was unusual in having two platforms, which were staggered but allowed trains to pass. It was a busy station serving a large village. (Lens of Sutton Association)

Board of Trade Inspector's report describes the following works. There were 58 aqueducts constructed over the marshy areas, supported on piles driven 40 to 50 ft into the ground, plus 23 road bridges, some of which had spans of over 60 ft. There were two viaducts over the rivers Tone (35 ft) and Parrett (47 ft), both tested by parking two locomotives on them and measuring the deflection at the centres ($\frac{3}{8}$ inch and $\frac{7}{16}$ inch respectively). There was one substantial cutting at the Yeovil end of the 18 mile journey.

The LSWR line arrived in 1860 and in 1861 the jointly owned Town station was opened, a grand building with a massive overall roof of glass built in a similar way to the Crystal Palace, but the platforms and railway facilities were minimal. The branch to Taunton was converted to mixed gauge in 1866, but as standard trains quickly outnumbered broad, the line was changed to only standard gauge in 1879. The section between Langport and

Athelney crossed the Somerset Levels and was always prone to flooding, only being improved in 1906 when this section became part of the GWR Westbury–Castle Cary–Taunton diversion route to the West Country. Langport station was renamed Langport West (a separate Langport East was opened on the new Westbury line). The station still flooded from time to time when the river Parrett overflowed. Though the branch trains ran on through Durston and over the four-track section to Taunton, our 'Lost' line ends at Curry Rivel junction where the main line still thunders north to Westbury and London.

Private sidings were put in around Hendford to serve the Petter factory (later Westland Aircraft) and another to the Bunford Flax Mill. Montacute station was added in 1882, and in 1885 a siding was provided for Mead & Son at Langport West. A loop was installed in 1927 at Thorney & Kingsbury to serve a Nestlé's Dairy milk depot. Both the GWR line south from Pen Mill and the LSWR link between the Town and Junction stations were doubled and in 1943 a double track link was put in between them to allow trains to run through from Pen Mill straight onto the SR Exeter line.

The larger stations all had goods yards, Hendford in particular, with a timber yard, cattle pens and a siding into a large stone works. A small passenger halt was opened near Hendford in 1932 to serve the growing industry on the Taunton side of the original station, which had long been just a goods depot.

The Westland Aircraft factory had its own rail system and engines with trucks being delivered and collected by the duty shunting engine, which worked all day around the various Yeovil stations.

The original passenger service consisted of five trains with two on Sundays, but this was reduced to four within a week! Goods services were started with coal and milk being important traffic. By 1886 the service was back to six trains, but they still terminated at Durston, where passengers for Taunton had to change. The operation of passenger trains between Yeovil Pen Mill and Town was designed to cater for passengers joining or leaving the GWR trains to and from Weymouth – you couldn't book a trip just between the two Yeovil stations!

Langport West had two platforms and a considerable goods yard, which can just be seen on the left hand edge of this picture, taken around 1912. Beyond the yard runs the river, which from time to time flooded the tracks. (Lens of Sutton Association)

Yeovil's stations included some strange arrangements. Pen Mill originally had a straightforward layout with two through lines and two platform lines; however, a fire caused the rebuilding of the down platform after which it was decided to use just the up platform! This was arranged as two sections end-on – not a unique idea in the early days. The problem was that there was no provision for a Weymouth-bound train to leave the platform and reach the correct line south. The train therefore had to reverse back northwards onto the single line and then set off again onto the correct line, passing as it went the disused platform. When trains were scheduled to pass each other at Pen Mill the two trains were allowed to drive into the one platform, engine to engine. Having completed loading, the southbound train reversed as before and once it was clear of the station the northbound train set off. As part of the elimination of the broad gauge tracks Yeovil Pen Mill was rebuilt, retaining the up platform but replacing the old down platform with an island platform that allowed more conventional passing of trains. Even now there was only a single line between the up platform and the new island platform, allowing passengers to leave the train on both sides.

Yeovil Junction was also rebuilt; the original station had two island platforms with a single track between them. The main line trains used the outside faces whilst the branch train to Yeovil Town worked from the central platform. The use of these double sided, single line platforms was supposed to enable knowledgeable passengers to get out on the right side of the carriage depending on which connection they intended to make. The new junction station took on a more modern shape with through lines down the centre, two loops serving the platforms and a bay platform for the branch train to the town.

Engines started with 4-2-2 Gooch tender locomotives but they were damaged by the poor track and the remainder of the broad gauge era was served by 4-4-0 saddle tanks. These were rather ugly brutes, with one driving axle being roughly in the centre of the loco and the other directly under the footplate. The steps to gain access to the footplate went over the wheel before one descended to the footplate level. Nevertheless, they worked right up to the end of the broad gauge era.

Locomotives were kept at both Pen Mill and Town stations, though Pen Mill normally served the Taunton branch. The Pen Mill route was always busy with a lot of trains coming from Weymouth docks, which handled much of the traffic from the Channel Isles. In the 20th century many of the common GWR branch line engines worked the line including Dean Goods, the Metro 2-4-0 tanks and the 272 class 0-6-0 saddle tanks. Many of the 2-6-2 tanks, panniers (many converted from old saddle tanks) and the delightful 1400 class 0-4-2s were used in the 1920 to 1940 period, with passenger trains now normally covering the whole route right through to Taunton. The 1957 timetable shows eight weekday trains taking between an hour and an hour and ten minutes for the journey.

Due in part to the mixture of three routes, plus the single track link between the Town and Pen Mill stations, there were a surprising number of accidents in Yeovil. The worst was at Pen

Mill in 1913, when a Weymouth express ran into the rear of an excursion train on the same line, fortunately at slow speed although three passengers died. Though the driver of the express was found guilty of neglect, there is no doubt that the branch line nature of the Yeovil stations, with their limited platforms and curves, couldn't handle the vastly increased traffic of the period.

A somewhat unusual accident occurred in 1914 when a goods train heading down the LSWR main line broke apart. The rear section of trucks caught up with the front section, smashing into them exactly outside the small west signal box, the wooden top half of which was pushed off its stone base and dumped precariously onto the top of the embankment. Luckily the signalman was not seriously injured.

During the 1920s to 1940s various attempts were made to challenge the inroads being made by lorries and buses. Two extra halts were opened and for a while a diesel railcar ran a non-stop service between Yeovil and Taunton. Excursion traffic was sought and added useful revenue, but everywhere the signs of the end could be seen.

Though attempts were made to reduce the number of men employed, much of the railway's work was still labour intensive, particularly the goods traffic. Yeovil Town, for instance, still employed 22 staff in 1923. Throughout the 1930 to 1960 period the railways were always playing 'catch up'; they failed to realise what passengers actually wanted until it was far too late. Goods traffic, for so long the mainstay of many rural lines, was moving to the roads. The ability to collect goods direct from the factories or farms and deliver them directly to the customers simply could not be matched by the railways. This was nobody's fault, it was just a fact of life.

The branch closed in 1964 and all traffic around Yeovil, except for the old GWR line from Frome to Weymouth, ended in 1968.

In the 1990s the Yeovil Railway Centre was established in the old Clifton Maybank sidings at the side of Yeovil Junction station. The centre provides servicing facilities for steam engines on rail tours in the area, plus occasional brake van rides along the route of the old broad gauge line; it also has a shop.

4
Yatton, the Junction for Nowhere

The Yatton to Clevedon branch
The Yatton to Blagdon branch –
the Wrington Vale Light Railway
The Yatton, Wells, Shepton Mallet
and Witham line

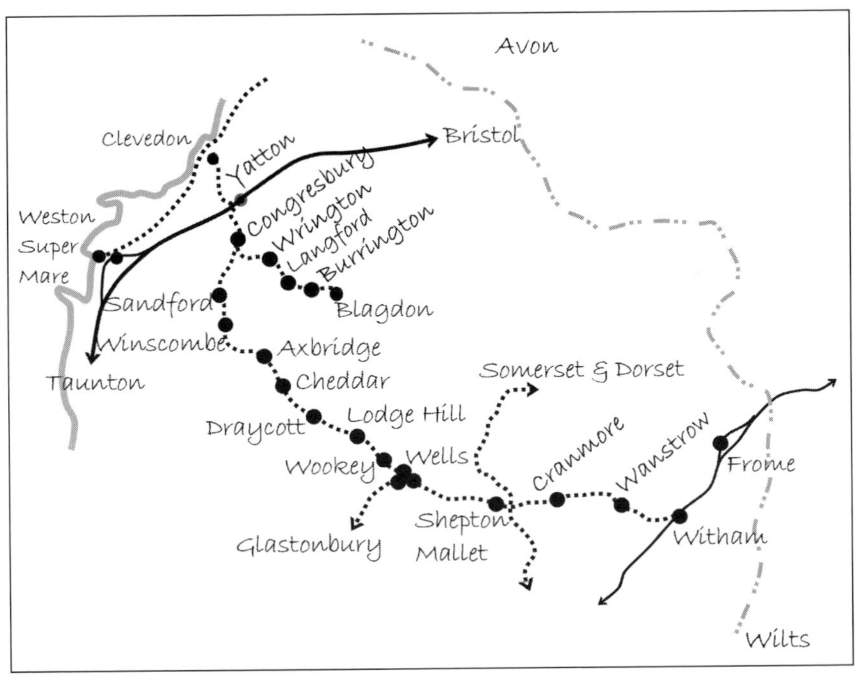

The Yatton to Clevedon branch

This once busy branch goes back to the very earliest days, being opened in 1847 as a broad gauge line and then standardised in 1879. At first the service was very modest, with just five weekday

trains and two on Sundays, but this steadily increased until by 1909 there were eighteen and four trains respectively. The service peaked in the 1950s when 26 weekday trains ran plus 10 on Sundays. Even in its final year there were still 23 trains on weekdays. Yatton was a busy junction with an engine shed and turntable, plus the usual sidings and goods yard. There were no intermediate stations and Clevedon station was re-laid in the 1880s after the change to standard gauge track. It had a goods shed, a small signal box, which became just a ground frame after 1917, and five sidings. One of these provided the connection to the Weston, Clevedon & Portishead line, which involved such a tight curve that it was always difficult to traverse and was not used after 1908.

The Clevedon branch left from a dedicated covered (until 1956) bay platform though there were connections to the main line platforms as well for the occasional through train from Bristol. The earliest locomotives were Bristol & Exeter 2-2-2 tanks. These

Yatton junction with the Clevedon train waiting in its own bay platform. Pannier tank No 5403 will shortly set off down the branch. (Author's Collection)

Clevedon station in 1960. The yard was to the left and the Weston, Clevedon & Portishead line passed left to right beyond the station building. (Lens of Sutton Association)

only had wooden block brakes acting on just the single driving wheels and great skill was needed, with careful use of reverse to slow the train down. The B&E also used a steam railmotor for a few years. Later, class 517 tanks were used and by the 1920s most trains were auto coaches using GWR tank engines, like the 1400 class or GWR railmotors. The last six years saw a DMU providing the service. After the demise of the Weston, Clevedon & Portishead line in 1940 the branch provided the coal for the Clevedon gasworks, though it had to be taken by cart from the station. This traffic reached over 12,000 tons in the 1940s and must have kept a modest sized lorry busy every day. Alas this traffic ended in 1951 and by 1963 all goods work ceased, followed by the passenger services in 1966.

The entire site is now a retail park and the only hint of its former function is this rail-built name post. (Author)

Yatton to Blagdon – the Wrington Vale Light Railway

The Wrington Vale Light Railway was born as the result of two needs – the necessity for farmers to market their dairy products quickly and the building, by the Bristol Corporation, of their new Yeo reservoir near Blagdon. An earlier scheme to build a line down the same valley to Blagdon and then on to Farrington Gurney on the existing Bristol to Frome line had been proposed in 1881. This had been well supported and by 1882 it had achieved its Act in parliament; however, the money could not be raised and the scheme came to naught.

Once the Light Railway Act had been passed in 1896 it awoke interest in failed minor railway ideas all over the country. Aided by local landowners and supported by Bristol and the GWR, a Light Railway Act was obtained to build the Wrington Vale Light Railway from a junction on the Yatton to Wells line to Blagdon, a distance of 6½ miles.

Congresbury station where the Blagdon line started. The junction is just visible in the far distance. (Author's Collection)

Wrington, seen here around 1912, was the principal station and served a large and important village. (Lens of Sutton Association)

During the public enquiry, Colonel E H Llewellyn, local MP, GWR director and leading proponent of the line, made a reply that would have today's health and safety people dumbstruck. Questions had been raised over the level crossings on the line and their safety to which Llewellyn commented, '*As to crossings, we must not expect too complicated and costly arrangements. That's not to say people must not mind being killed now and then, but I feel that the Great Western Railway will take every precaution for the safe working of the railway.*'

Constructed by the GWR it opened in 1901 to the usual local celebrations. It is interesting to realise just how much a railway connection meant even as late as the beginning of the 20th century. Yatton station had opened in 1841 and Congresbury in 1869, these being just a few miles away from Wrington, the main village on our line. In the days before refrigeration even these small distances were a problem for the dairy farmers who had to get their products to the large cities as soon as possible.

When the line opened the local children were given a day off from school and taken on a free trip. The first trains were greeted

Langford station in this nicely posed postcard shot from around 1912. (Lens of Sutton Association)

at each station by enthusiastic crowds, and out of the local population of around 3,000 nearly 1,000 people travelled on the first day. In 1904 there was an attempt to extend the line to the Bristol–Frome line near Pensford, but despite the considerable coal seams in the area this wasn't progressed. The line settled down and quietly served its purpose but by 1920 bus and road competition was cutting into its revenue and in 1931 the passenger service ended, one of the earliest in the West Country.

Just how local industry could grow around a station is well illustrated by the village of Wrington. The Organ Brothers were upholstery manufacturers and saddlers who received flock from Bristol and Exeter by rail. Their bridles and saddles left by train, with horse collars being packed in hessian bales. At least six milk churns left each day, though at over 2 cwt each the farmer had to contract others to provide assistance for their loading. Coal naturally featured, with Messrs Clements still receiving three wagons a day in 1950. Lynham's, the bakers, collected flour by horse and cart, Walters, the millers, collected grain and the local farmers collected cattle cake and sugar beet pulp feedstuffs.

Blagdon in 1925, a tidy station near the new lake but with a very steep climb up to the village. (Brunel University/Mowat Collection)

Today the station is a private residence but the platform and station have been preserved. (Author)

Trains ran to and from Yatton and a service of four trains a day plus one goods train was provided at the start, which increased to five by 1903, plus a single train on Sundays. By 1930 only two trains were running, with no Sunday service. Though short, the line included a half mile section at 1 in 50, which must have woken up the little 517 class 0-4-2 tank engines that operated the line. The coaches were four-wheeled, with usually three coaches forming the set. These worked right through until the end of the passenger service, by which time they were some of the last four-wheel coaches left on the GWR. Between 1908 and the early 1930s a steam railmotor was used on certain trains, sharing its duties with the Clevedon branch.

There were no signals as the line operated on a 'one engine in steam' rule. At Blagdon there was a spur to a coal store provided for the steam water pumps associated with the reservoir. Nearby was the home of Sir W.H. Wills and the area was known as Imperial Valley, acknowledging the local wealth derived from tobacco. His Coombe Lodge estate has its own small siding used, among other things, for transporting the shire horses for which the estate was famous.

Ever declining goods traffic lingered on, worked by various 0-4-2 locos and even ex-LMS class 2 Ivatt 2-6-2s, until the end section between Wrington and Blagdon was closed in 1950, followed by the remainder in 1963. That the track remained usable for so long after the passenger service ended, shows how devoid the area was of main roads or expanding villages craving for a bypass, which would have snatched up the old trackbed without hesitation.

The Yatton, Wells, Shepton Mallet and Witham line

This line was formed from two independent broad gauge lines, the first from Witham to Wells and the second from Yatton to Wells. The first started as a branch, opened in 1856, from the

Yatton junction again, but this time showing the whole station, taken in 1912. The Wells line used the far bay platform, behind the water tower. (Lens of Sutton Association)

Frome–Yeovil line. It left at Witham and headed into the hilly area around Shepton Mallet, which it reached in 1858. Four years later this had been extended into Wells. The other line was a branch opened by the Bristol & Exeter company from its main line junction at Yatton to Cheddar in 1869, and a year later it too reached Wells (Tucker Street). As described in the Somerset & Dorset chapter, the S&D line from Glastonbury had reached Wells in 1859. Each line had its own terminus giving Wells three stations, and three different companies, with the two broad gauge lines staring at each other across the standard gauge S&D station.

The GWR had absorbed the Bristol & Exeter along with its Yatton branches in 1876, and had also absorbed the East Somerset company, leaving two GWR stations separated by the S&D track. Both lines had also been converted to standard gauge. Two years later the problems of crossing the S&D goods yard were resolved and the three stations were joined. The GWR now reduced the former East Somerset station to goods only and Tucker Street became the GWR station with trains running over the S&D tracks and through Priory Road station. Passengers wanting to travel from the S&D line to stations on the GWR line had to walk from

Congresbury with a pannier 8746 shunting a mixed goods train from Wells and beyond. (R.E. Toop)

PASSENGERS ARE REQUESTED
TO CROSS THE LINE
AT THE OTHER END
OF THE PLATFORM

Winscombe station around 1910, looking busy and tidy. (Lens of Sutton Association)

Winscombe station today, now a footpath. A novel feature is a timeline, which starts just to the right of the camera in year 0 and goes right up to date at the far end of the well preserved platform edge. (Author)

Priory Road station to the GWR Tucker Street station. Eventually in 1934 both the S&D and the GWR trains used Priory Road station until the S&D branch closed in 1951; thereafter the old GWR Tucker Street station (now just called Wells) was used until the closure of the Yatton–Witham line passenger service in 1963.

There was a large paper mill at Wookey, which had rail connections until 1965 and, along with quarry products from Dulcote Quarry, provided local freight traffic through to the Witham end of the line. Virtually all the stations had goods facilities to handle the necessary coal and agricultural needs of the area. Locomotives included the usual GWR branch line 2-6-2 tanks, pannier tanks and ex-LMS 0-4-4 tanks plus class 2 BR 2-6-0s, often with just one or two coaches. Diesel railcars started in the 1930s and were used right into the 1950s. Apart from visiting specials, DMUs don't seem to have been used on the line. The gradients east of Wells were extremely hard going, with 3 miles at 1 in 47 to reach Shepton Mallet. Further lengths of around the

Cheddar station with the typical GWR overall roof, photographed in 1949. The station is now used by the Wells Cathedral Stonemasons. (J. Moss)

Axbridge station in the early 1950s, looking towards Wells. In the season this station was busy with the strawberry traffic. (J. Moss)

This shot is taken from almost the same spot! The trackbed and left hand platform are now under the Axbridge bypass. (Author)

Draycott station in 1960, now a private residence. It was well placed at the bottom of the village and originally had a small goods yard. (Lens of Sutton Association)

1 in 50 mark were encountered before Witham was reached, making the strong 2-6-2 tanks popular with the crews.

Passenger services were generally around five to seven trains on weekdays and after 1900 a single Sunday mixed train ran, though its main purpose was the milk traffic. The journey time in the 1950s was around the 1½ hours mark for the 31½ miles.

It is very easy to get the idea that branch lines romped along until the 1960s when wicked scheming put an untimely end to it all. Often the passenger services peaked in the 1930s, again reinforcing the all-was-well image but, if we look at the actual figures, it tells a different story. The Cheddar line served some good sized towns, in most cases the stations were well positioned, and it had a potential bonus in the tourist trade. If we look at the figures for Shepton Mallet (High Street) station, we see typical figures which can leave nobody in doubt that things were not well.

Wookey station in 1960. The point once fed the goods shed but by this time only served the adjacent paper mill. Note the way the signal box was placed forward in order to see under the road bridge. (Lens of Sutton Association)

Wookey today with the goods shed and the paper mill beyond, both still working long after the line closed. (Author)

Wells Tucker Street, looking back towards Yatton. Another example of a former broad gauge line with the centre space being used for water columns at each end. The goods yard was beyond the road bridge though today it has nearly all vanished beneath a new bypass road. (Kidderminster Railway Museum)

Restored typical local wagon from the Wells area. (Author)

Shepton Mallet GWR station was well placed for the town. The buildings are quite different in style to the Yatton–Wells section, an indication of the original different company. (Lens of Sutton Association)

	1903	1913	1923	1933
Passenger tickets sold	29,631	25,010	18,584	6,308
Parcels forwarded	24,139	23,144	16,935	15,924
General goods forwarded (tons)	16,580	15,121	835	462
Materials received (Incl coal)	22,557	21,747	9,844	4,606

The Yatton–Wells section had always been the most successful, boosted by tourists to the Cheddar area. Prior to 1939 large quantities of milk were sent to London, along with strawberry traffic in the season plus, of course, cheese. The inevitable camping coaches appeared at many of the smaller stations in the

Cranmore station in the 1960s. The sidings on the right originally served granite quarries but were later extended behind the station for bitumen trains, which ran until 1985. (Lens of Sutton Association)

Now restored and home to the East Somerset Railway a ex-Yugoslav 0-6-0 arrives with a train of trippers in 2007. (Author)

Wanstrow station served its nearby village well but was never going to save the line. Today gravel trains run through from the Merehead quarry en route to the main line. (Lens of Sutton Association)

1930s and lasted until the end. In 1963 the line closed except for the section from Yatton to Cheddar serving a private siding until 1969. At the Witham end of the line, freight traffic continued to Cranmore for bitumen and quarry products from Foster Yeomans extensive works via a new rail link. Foster Yeomans were the first private owner of main line diesels (using four General Motors (USA) locomotives), which were driven and maintained by British Rail.

In 1975 David Shepherd opened his steam centre at Cranmore and in 1980 was running trains over a short section from a new station called Cranmore West towards Shepton Mallet. When the bitumen traffic ended in 1985 the steam service returned to the, then vacant, original Cranmore station and was extended to Mendip Vale nearer to Shepton Mallet, giving a 2 mile line. Known as the East Somerset Railway it operates a service of steam-hauled trains throughout the summer season.

Stone traffic still runs from the Merehead quarry to Witham and onto the main line.

5
Mendip Wanderings

The Bristol, Radstock and Frome line
The Camerton branch and
The Titfield Thunderbolt
The Weston, Clevedon & Portishead Railway

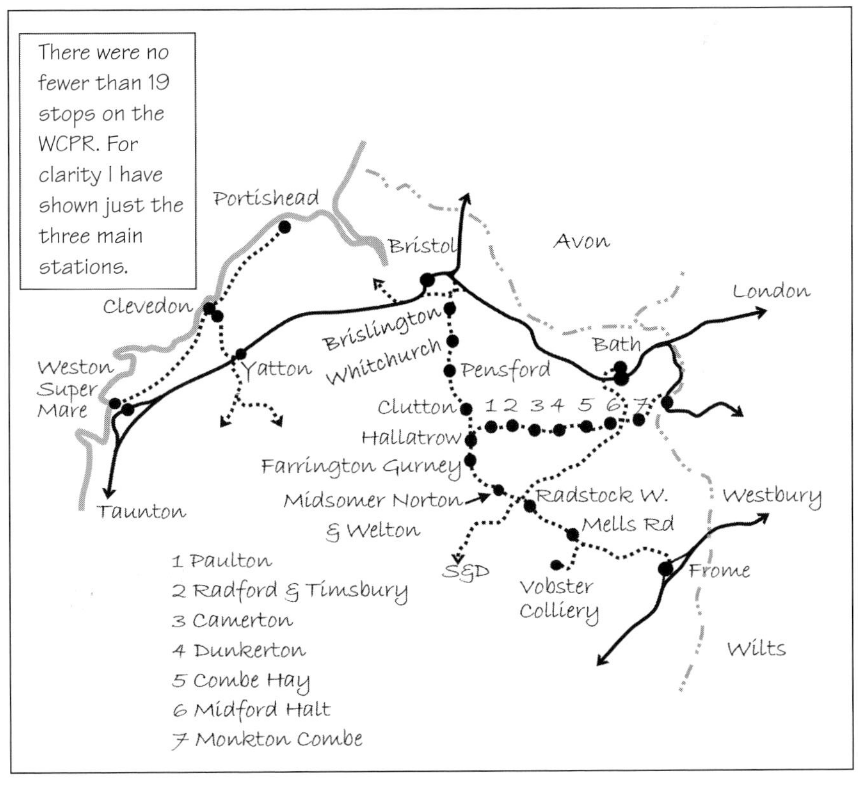

The Bristol, Radstock and Frome line

The Somerset coalfields comprised some 80 collieries, though never all working at the same time. The coal seams were relatively thin and like the surrounding land far from straight or flat, indeed even in the 1940s only a third of the coal was being cut by machine. Production varied from nearly 1½ million tons in 1900 when some 10,000 men were employed to around ½ million tons per year in the 1950s, when just 3,000 men were still at work. Though much of the coal was used locally, movement of coal was a major income for the area's railways.

Yet again our line came into being as two lines, the older being a broad gauge branch opened from Frome in 1854, built primarily for the coal traffic from Radstock. The second part was formed by the standard gauge Bristol & North Somerset Railway, opened in 1873 and headed towards Radstock from Bristol. This was again motivated by coal, which was abundant in the Radstock area.

Mells Road, the first station from Frome, where for many years various collieries and quarries in the area had links to the main line. (Lens of Sutton Association)

Midsomer Norton & Welton station in 1962. Goods here included explosives for the collieries. After closure the building burnt down and the site is now completely gone. (Lens of Sutton Association)

Just a year later the broad gauge line was converted to standard gauge. This was the same year that saw the Somerset & Dorset line open, again through Radstock. Through passenger trains between Bristol and Frome began to run in 1875. Both lines ran close to each other and the two Radstock stations were just a few hundred yards apart. These two stations seem to have been known by their line, ie S&D or GWR, rather than by separate names , though the GWR station certainly became Radstock West and one reference shows the S&D station as Radstock North.

In 1884 the Bristol & North Somerset became part of the GWR and the line was worked as a single through route. Except for a short section south of Radstock the line was single track throughout.

Hallatrow around 1925, junction for the Camerton line, which can be seen turning right behind the goods shed. Always busy with coal trains in particular, the site is now a factory estate. (Author's Collection)

As one would expect from a line that runs through the Mendip Hills there were almost no level sections. For the first 2 miles from Frome the gradients stayed fairly easy and the line dropped very slightly into the river Frome valley, but from here to the outskirts of Bristol the line was either climbing or descending a series of four summits. Gradients as steep as 1 in 48 with many miles at 1 in 60 or 70 faced the locomotive and driver on their journey to Bristol.

We'll take a journey north from Frome where the line formed a triangular junction just north of Frome station, from which the single line set off in a north-westerly direction, soon passing the gasworks with its siding. Next came the first of the quarry lines, originally a 2 ft gauge tramway to the Vallis Vale quarry, converted to standard gauge in 1943 and later extended to the Whatley quarry. At Mells Road two more lines are met, the oldest, the Newbury Railway from 1858, was a broad gauge feeder for coal and limestone, later to be known as the Vobster branch. A shorter line, the Mells Quarry Railway, ran from an exchange siding to the Mells quarry and was active between 1925 to 1934, when this quarry was joined to the Newbury system, which itself lasted until 1994. Parts were reopened in 1968 and used until 1982.

Approaching Radstock, we can be in no doubt as to what was the main industry. Lines, some narrow, come down to exchange sidings from Huish, Writhlington and Kilmersdon collieries, long coal wagon sidings are everywhere and the Radstock wagon works looms up on the left. Just ½ mile before the town's station four lines sweep away to the north to Ludlows Colliery. A single siding left these colliery sidings and fed several other works including the British Wagon Works and a rarely used connection to the S&D line for the transfer of wagons. The station was in the centre of the town with the Somerset & Dorset line's station just to the north. Both lines crossed over the High Street on level crossings, causing endless traffic jams.

Clutton station, looking back towards Frome around 1910. The sidings were mainly used for coal wagons. (Lens of Sutton Association)

Pensford Viaduct today, still proudly standing long after any trains have crossed it. At 330 yds long it was by far the largest structure on the line. (Author)

Pensford station in the early 1960s with the passing loop gone. The goods shed remained in use until 1964. (Lens of Sutton Association)

Brislington station always had just the one platform. Note the distinctive chimneys used on all the stations on the line except Mells Road. (Lens of Sutton Association)

West of the next station, Midsomer Norton & Welton, came yet more collieries – Old Mills and Springfield. Again the station names seem to have a life of their own as this station was originally Welton, then Welton & Midsomer Norton and finally as above. Next came Farrington Gurney Halt where tickets were issued from a small office beneath a water tank at the rear of the local pub – that's what I call a rural railway! North of Hallatrow station was the junction for the Camerton branch, followed by the Cloud Hill quarry. Clutton had two long sidings, one to Fry's Bottom Colliery while the other, over a mile long, served Greyfield Colliery. There was also another wagon works here. Between here and Pensford a line arrived from Pensford Colliery to which yet another colliery was connected by a 2 ft tramway, both working into the 1950s. Pensford station, reached after crossing the 330 yd long viaduct, was the least busy station on the line. Whitchurch had a lowly halt with just a simple pagoda style shed. The last station, Brislington, was virtually a suburb of

In memory of Hallatrow station, the only clue remaining of the railway. (Author)

Bristol and had to contend with the main housing area being well served by trams from the early 1910s. The approach to Bristol Temple Meads was, as always, contorted and, in the days of steam, exciting.

Passenger services started with just five trains plus two on Sundays, which grew slowly to around eight plus three respectively. One train, which connected at Frome with the London-bound Channel Island boat train, ran fast, only stopping at Radstock and Pensford en route to Bristol.

Passenger services ended in 1959 with goods traffic carrying on north of Radstock, and from quarries near Mells Road south to

Frome. In 1970 a short section of the old S&D line from Writhlington Colliery was linked to the Frome line just west of the Radstock stations to allow coal to be taken out by train. The last coal train left Radstock in 1973 but the line remained open to the Radstock wagon works until 1988. The southern quarry traffic still runs today.

The Camerton branch and
The Titfield Thunderbolt

Coal was again the reason this delightful little line was built – firstly in 1882 as a 3½ mile branch from Hallatrow on the Bristol–Frome line to Camerton. The gradients were fairly steep and coal

Camerton station with coal wagons around 1910. Though passenger services ended in 1925 the line remained down into the 1950s. (Lens of Sutton Association)

Dunkerton station in a rather gloomy shot taken in 1930 when only coal trains ran. The colliery, once the largest in the area, was some way back towards Camerton. (Brunel University/Mowat Collection)

trains were limited to 15 wagons. In 1907 the line was extended to Dunkerton Colliery and finally in 1910 to the Trowbridge–Bathampton line near Limpley Stoke. This last section used part of the old Somerset Coal Canal including the Combe Hay tunnel.

The line leaves Hallatrow, turning east and dropping down ¼ mile at 1 in 47 before we reach Paulton Halt, nearly a mile from the village; opened in 1914 just in time to be closed in 1915! Next comes Radford & Timsbury Halt, which boasted a brick station building with a passing loop and, more importantly, a 600 yd long siding to the nearby Lower Conygre Colliery. This originally had a narrow gauge incline down to the Somerset Coal Canal, the old course of which winds near the railway line. Next comes Camerton, provided with sidings including extensive lines around the Camerton New Colliery, which worked until 1950. The old colliery, near the station, closed in 1898 but was connected to the new pit by underground workings. Next is Dunkerton Colliery Halt built to serve the colliery, which had two shafts and for a while was the largest in the Somerset coalfields. Dunkerton station soon follows with a passing loop and small yard. By Combe Hay Halt the line is built over the old canal bed and uses the original canal tunnel.

There was a long lost Midford Halt; Midford is where our line nips under the viaduct that carries the Somerset & Dorset line northwards. This was the spot used for the opening scenes in *The Titfield Thunderbolt*, the classic Ealing Comedy film made in 1952 about a community's fight to save its railway. The last branch station comes at Monkton Combe, a basic station with a passing loop and a single siding, but which was at least near the village.

Monkton Combe in happier days. The line was virtually on top of the old canal at this point and the trackbed can be walked towards Limpley Stoke. (Lens of Sutton Association)

Monkton Combe was used as 'Titfield' station for the film. This last section was again built over the old canal, including the last half a mile through Combe Hay tunnel and onto the curving embankment that led to the GWR's Bradford on Avon line. Following half a mile running parallel to the 'main' line, it arrives at Limpley Stoke station where it had its own bay platform.

Through passenger services ran from Hallatrow, through Camerton and on to Limpley Stoke but they only lasted until 1915. Public pressure got the service started again in 1923 but it lasted for just two more years, until 1925.

A single coach was all that was needed, usually added to a coal train until around 1910 when an autotrain with a 517 class 0-4-2 tank engine was used. There were five down trains but strangely only three up. The link to the Bristol–Frome branch closed first, with all track removed. The collieries closed one by one until 1950 when all were gone. The last general goods train ran in 1951, after which came the line's moment of glory when the track was used for the making of *The Titfield Thunderbolt* film. The remaining track was finally lifted in 1958.

The Weston, Clevedon & Portishead Railway

Originally intended to be a steam-hauled tramway, this opened in 1897 as a conventional standard gauge railway. So slow was the construction that the Act covering the section to Portishead had lapsed and a new one was needed, which included a change to the name by adding 'Light' before 'Railway', though it never operated under a Light Railway Order. Following a protracted dispute with the Clevedon District Council over a level crossing, the line opened to Portishead in 1907. In 1904 the original company was taken over but soon went into liquidation and that gallant saviour of small lines, Colonel Stephens, took over. Colonel Stephens undertook the management of many 'lost' branch lines, imposing a spartan regime which kept them

Weston super Mare, pictured in the early 1930s. The offices were in the round roofed building on the left. The track was a bare minimum but included a siding beyond the platform. (Lens of Sutton Association)

running well into the 1930s. After his death in 1931 losses were still being made and the service stopped in 1939 on the outbreak of war, the receiver closing the railway in 1940. The GWR purchased the track for use as a storage siding but never in fact used it and in 1942 it was lifted.

The station at Weston was a very modest affair with just a run round loop and two small sidings. The platform had a little shelter and a solitary gaslight; built entirely of wood it looked as if it might not be too safe to walk on! The main building had the

Worle Town Halt around 1934 with a siding just beyond the level crossing. This photo catches the ambience of this lovely little line. Worle today is completely consumed by housing and supermarkets. (Brunel University/Mowat Collection)

appearance of a corrugated iron farm building. It was situated some ¾ mile from the pier, to which the company ran a horse-drawn bus in the early years. They had originally laid a short length of tramway along the road towards the pier in the early tramway days but had to remove it when they became a light railway. There were a further nine stations between Weston and Clevedon, all minus platforms but with simple shelters. About halfway along, the line crossed over the inlet of the river Yeo, which was just big enough to handle small vessels when the tide was right. A spur was built onto a wooden jetty, which allowed trans-shipment of coal, the wagons being moved by a converted Fordson tractor. Clevedon station included the main workshops and was the headquarters of the line. The platform though, like Weston, was of all wooden construction with a simple shelter. The booking office was again a curved roof, agricultural style building on the 'wrong' side of the line. Passengers had to get their tickets then walk back to the road in order to cross over the line, then walk back to the platform along a fenced path.

The section from Clevedon through Walton in Gordano was along the northern side of a beautiful valley known locally as 'Swiss Valley'. Today the southern side of this valley carries the M5 as it climbs Tickenham Hill. On the route to Portishead there

A typical mixed train near Clevedon pulled by a former London–Brighton Terrier 0-6-0 in 1935. This loco had previously been the Littlehampton Wharf Shunter. (Brunel University/Clinker Collection)

Clevedon included the workshops and headquarters of the line. The station itself is to the left in this picture from the 1930s. The two coaches were built by the Lancaster Carriage and Wagon works in 1897. (Lens of Sutton Association)

are three quarries, the first being fed by a siding from the main line. The other two, Black Rock and Nightingale, had their own internal 2 ft gauge railway system, which was raised above the WCPR line and could tip the stones into WCPR wagons below. At Portishead there was the usual single platform, though this time the station building was adjacent to the platform and of a slightly more conventional shape. A siding fed into the Mustad Nail factory and from the run round loop the line continued across the road and into the exchange sidings with the GWR Portishead branch. This link carried the coal for Clevedon gasworks for many years.

The line used a miscellany of locomotives – two elderly 2-2-2 well tanks, a Manning Wardle 0-4-2, which was later converted to a 0-6-0, two ex-Brighton Terrier 0-6-0 tank engines and a selection of old coaches.

There was a connection to the GWR Clevedon branch via a very tight radius curve between the two goods yards, which proved a problem to use and was removed in 1908. To the east of the station the line crossed two streets – the cause of the eruptions with the council – before reaching the goods yard and a small junction which fed a long siding to the gasworks. These works consumed some 5,000 tons of coal in the early 1900s, which rose steadily to over 7,000 tons by the time the line closed.

The line served mostly request stops on its 14 mile journey and one suspects that speed was not too important. Basically two engines were in use in summer, providing between six and eight trips, and one in winter when only three journeys were made. Stone wagons from the quarries between Clevedon and Portishead were added to the passenger trains as necessary. For a long time a Dewry petrol railcar was also used on the busier Clevedon to Weston section.

Another Terrier loco (No 2) at Portishead with two coaches. The platform was very low and hidden by the train. Low platforms or more usually no platform at all was the reason for the steps. (Lens of Sutton Association)

6
Lines Around Bristol

The Portishead branch
Lines within Bristol
The Avonmouth area
The Bristol & South Wales Union Railway

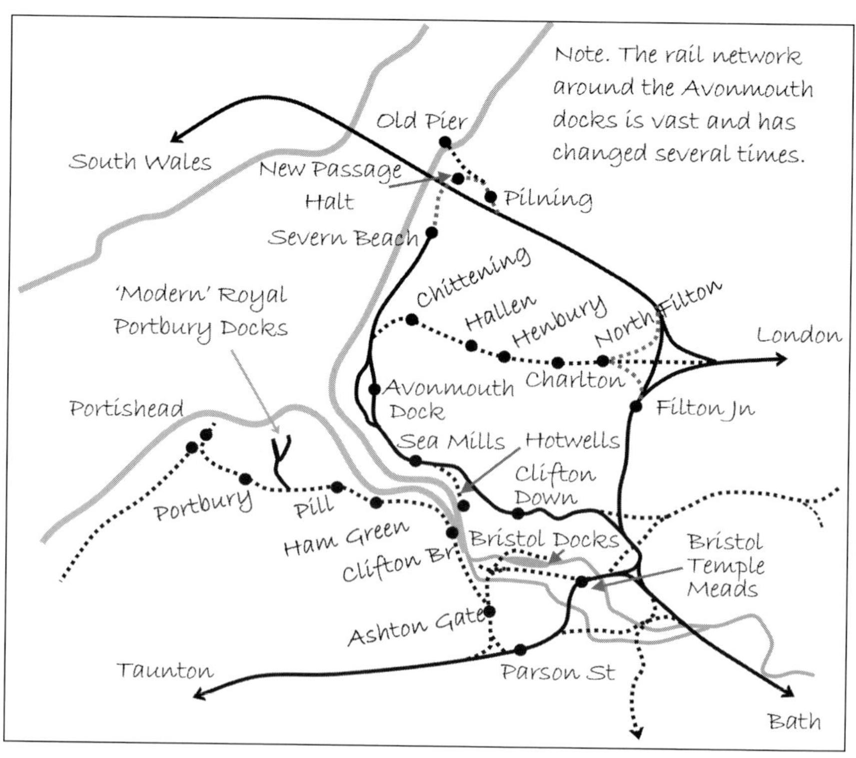

The Portishead branch

This line is only partly 'lost' as freight from the docks around Portbury is still moved by rail, but passenger traffic ended in 1964. The history of this line is bound up in the endless debates that raged in Bristol during the 19th century. The city was, of course, long known for its shipbuilding and worldwide trading. In 1809 William Jessop had completed the Floating Harbour, which gave Bristol a deep water tide-free area where ships could load and unload their cargoes. The approach to the harbour was via locks from the river Avon, which in turn could be navigated at high tide from the river Severn estuary. It was the limitations of having to use the relatively narrow Avon gorge that caused the forward-looking merchants of the town to seek better harbour facilities. There were two approaches; one favoured the north side of the Avon as it entered the Severn, the other the south side.

The first station after leaving the main line is Ashton Gate where the line into Bristol Harbour departed on the right. (Lens of Sutton Association)

Clifton Bridge station, named for its location but not for its use as a way to reach the bridge! Again we can see the former broad gauge gap between the lines in this shot from the 1930s. (Lens of Sutton Association)

These two factions plus the diehard Bristol harbour men argued the merits of their schemes for years. All manner of plans were put forward including damming the gorge to form a series of harbours. In 1862 a line along the north side of the Avon obtained its Act and work began.

This fired up the supporters of the south side scheme who formed the Bristol & Portishead Pier & Railway Company, which obtained its Act in 1863 and four years later the broad gauge line was opened. The line was to leave the main Bristol & Exeter line and head north to Portbury where docks would be built. A branch was proposed to Portishead in order to serve the small village that was already well established there. As the building progressed several changes were made to the route and the Portbury line was quietly dropped; instead the Portishead area would be developed with a new quay and pier.

Clifton Bridge station site today. Goods traffic from the Royal Portbury Docks keeps the line open. (Author)

The construction was quite difficult for such a modest line. There were tunnels and a long curving wooden viaduct that crossed a tidal inlet just before reaching Portishead. After the usual minor adjustments imposed by the Board of Trade inspector were completed, the line opened in April 1867. Though now ready for business the company was in financial trouble, the costs having been well over £200,000 – there was not even money to spare to celebrate the opening. During the building, both the rival Avonmouth line and the Clifton Suspension Bridge had been completed. The pier at Portishead was extended just three years later and steamer services began running to Cardiff, Swansea and Ilfracombe. We must note that the rival line on the north side of the gorge only ran to Hotwells, just short of the Clifton bridge and still nearly a mile from Bristol city. It was not linked to the Bristol rail system until 1885 so the Portishead line had the monopoly of through traffic for some 18 years.

The Portishead company obtained an Act in 1871 to build a floating dock next to the Portishead station, connected to the Severn estuary by a single lock. In the same year the rival Avonmouth company received its Act to build docks at Avonmouth. Following a Board of Trade examination it was felt that there was sufficient trade to justify both docks and that the Bristol Corporation should consider investing in them. In the event, Portishead won the vote and received the corporation's £100,000. At the same time the locks to the original Bristol floating dock were rebuilt, so the scene was set for the rivalry to continue unabated. During the building of the docks both schemes met with problems but the Avonmouth docks faired better, opening for trade in 1877 whilst Portishead battled on until 1879 before its dock was ready.

Like the Clevedon branch the Portishead line had been operated by the Bristol & Exeter company, which became part of the GWR in 1876. Following yet more debate it was agreed in 1883 that both the Portishead and Avonmouth docks should be bought out by the Bristol Corporation, and as part of the same package the GWR were to take over the line. Some idea of just how difficult times were for both docks can be gauged from the prices paid. From costs of over £700,000 for the Avonmouth docks,

Pill station; the steps ran down to the platforms from the road. This was the only station to serve a self-contained village on the route to Portishead. (Lens of Sutton Association)

Another then and now shot. The station today photographed from the bridge above. (Author)

Bristol paid £450,000. The Portishead docks were costed at £375,000 and £250,000 was accepted. So in just five years, between 1879 and 1884, our line went from a dock-owning, independent company, glaring across the Avon at its rival, to being part of the GWR with the docks owned by the council and all rivalry gone!

The Portishead line was re-laid with standard gauge track in 1880 and in 1906 the junction from the main line was made into a vast triangle within which a goods depot and carriage storage sidings were built. At the same time a new link was built across the river Avon and into the Canons Marsh goods complex.

The first few miles of the journey are through the suburbs of Bristol, with Bedminster and Parson Street stations being on the main line to Taunton and Exeter. At Parson Street junction the branch leaves to the right and heads north through Ashton Gate and into Clifton Bridge station. Ashton was once a centre of coal mining but even when this had gone there were still coke, brick and metal works around the area, all with sidings to the branch. Just before the little Ashton Gate station is the junction to lines built in 1906 to reach the Bristol Harbour area. Sidings here were in use until 1987 for coal, and to 1991 for the civil engineering department.

Clifton Bridge station sits at the bottom of the Avon valley next to the river and in sight of the famous bridge. On the other bank is the lock that lifts boats from the tidal river Avon into the Bristol floating harbour. It was the inadequacy of these docks plus the nuisance of manoeuvring down the relatively narrow Avon gorge that led to the development of the Portishead and Avonmouth docks. Continuing north, now on a single line, we pass through three short tunnels between which are three narrow gauge quarry lines that ran under the branch line and into loading stages set into the river's edge. Beyond Ham Green Halt is Pill tunnel, some 665 yds long, and Pill station, which had a small goods yard and coal depot. Beyond Pill is the site of the branch to the abortive Portbury Shipyard, started in 1917 but abandoned in 1921. We now pass what today is the entrance to the modern coal and car loading sidings at the Royal Portbury Docks, more of which in a moment.

We are now on the truly lost part of the line at Portbury station. The village was ½ mile away and only had a population of 400. (Lens of Sutton Association)

We are now on the part of the branch that today is totally closed, first Portbury station and then Portishead. The dock at Portishead expanded over the years, attracting granaries, a large timber wharf, a gasworks and a chemical works, all served by rail, plus in 1926 a rail-fed, coal-fired power station, which used coal from the Radstock area for some time. During the 1914–18 war the petrol depot was expanded, handling vast quantities along with distilling Toluol, used in TNT. The Shell company had distilled this product in Rotterdam, but moved the entire distillery to Portishead where it was erected and back in production within just six weeks. The station had extensive goods yards, including the interchange sidings with the Weston, Clevedon & Portishead line.

The 1930s saw continued expansion and the introduction of a very good passenger service along the line, but the docks were not doing well and closure was considered in 1938. The Second World War, however, provided much work for the docks and the

Portishead station. The right hand platform was opened in 1930 and the coal-fired power station in the distance, above the station canopy, was opened in 1927. The engine shed, on the right, ceased to be used around 1900 and may have dated from the broad gauge days. (J.H. Moss)

line. Passenger services carried on, with the line taking people out of Bristol each evening to avoid the bombing raids and returning them the next morning. Following the war both passenger and goods traffic continued but like everywhere else the car and the lorry were now eating into the railway's work. As so often, it seems that British Rail did all it could to discourage rail traffic, though in fairness the figures often show this to have been due to simple economics rather than some strange suicidal tendency. After the war, coal came in for the power station in colliers from South Wales, with up to seven ships in and out on every tide.

The dock is now a marina and the old station area became a second power station, which started in 1954 when a new passenger station was built nearer to Portishead village. The old coal power station continued until 1976 and the 'new' Portishead rail station lasted until 1964 for passengers and 1967 for goods.

The new station, which was much nearer the village, produced a brief increase in passengers but having been built on ashes over mud it suffered from subsidence until the end.

The closure includes two odd tales. When British Rail decided to close the line, the National Dock Labour Board was consulted but replied that the dock workers had long deserted the railway and went to work by car! The second rather nice story involves the then Minister of Transport, Ernest Marples. Many West Country holiday lines were scheduled for closure in the winter of 1964 but he announced in the Commons that, to avoid spoiling any holiday arrangements that people may have already made, he was delaying the closures until the autumn. This affected both the Barnstaple and Minehead lines as well as Portishead.

All lay derelict until 2002 when new sidings, referred to above, were installed to serve the Royal Portbury Docks. These dock lines consist of two areas – a coal loading terminal fed by a ½ mile long conveyer from the ships and a car loading and general cargo area. Three long sidings run alongside a massive vehicle storage

Typical Portishead transport, though this one has been fully restored. (Author)

area, where cars are loaded onto double decker wagons to be transported to major centres throughout the British Isles. The new traffic generated required much of the old branch to be re-laid and even the floor of Pill tunnel had to be lowered to give a larger clearance for the coal and car transporters.

Quite an adventurous life for a 9 mile long branch line!

The branch was worked by the Bristol & Exeter from the start. Initially six weekday trains ran with just one on Sundays but, as one would expect, the railway brought prosperity to the district and by the late 1920s there were twenty-one weekday trains and eight on Sundays.

Railmotors were used, sometimes with an unpowered trailer coach; elderly 2-4-0 tender engines also featured in the 1920s and the delightful GWR railcars ran into the 1950s. Pannier tanks and standard BR tanks were also regular workers. The inevitable DMUs ran to the end in 1964.

Trains ran from Bristol Temple Meads at half hour intervals for most of the day. One service was known as the 'coast to coast', running from Severn Beach, through Avonmouth and into Bristol, then carrying on to the Portishead branch. After the war the service barely reached half the pre-war figures and by the last year of passenger service there were just six weekday trains. Today Portishead has become a vibrant town with modern apartment blocks looking over the marina and new building work going on where once the timber sheds stood. A modern commuter service would be so successful if only there was the will to re-lay the track and rebuild a new station.

Lines within Bristol

Like all large cities Bristol was targeted by several railway companies, each having its own station and goods yard. Add to that the docks and it is easy to imagine the fairly complex network that resulted. Originally the GWR from London terminated here, as did the Bristol & Exeter company plus the Midland Railway, which made its entrance from the north.

Before the lines from Ashton Gate could reach the harbour they had to cross over the river Avon and the docks. This swing bridge, with twin rail tracks below and a road on top, crossed the Avon. (Brunel University/Mowat Collection)

The swing bridge today. The lower deck carries a footpath and a long out of use single rail. The road deck and the control tower have all gone. (Author)

The bridge in its full glory in 1930. Very few ships used the tidal Avon at this point and the bridge was rarely swung. (Brunel University/Clinker Collection)

A similar view today. It's quite impossible to visualise what it originally looked like. Alas, Bristol has not provided any interpretation board to enlighten those who now stroll across the pathway. (Author)

Part of the dockside, by the Industrial Museum. The lines behind the camera originally passed under St Mary's church and into Temple Meads goods yard. (Author)

The lines strictly within the city are around the floating dock. This is a rather strange name for what is a river-fed basin in the heart of the city; what makes it unusual is its size plus the locks that allow ships to enter and leave via the tidal river Avon. The whole basin is some 2½ miles long and though now almost entirely used for leisure it was once the centre of the city's trading. Surprisingly, despite several schemes, the docks didn't have a rail connection until 1872, many decades after the docks opened. There are two groups of lines; one which led to the massive Canons Marsh goods depot and the other running along the southern side of the harbour. This fed many of the basins and warehouses and eventually joined into the rail system to the north of Temple Meads station.

The westerly feed to both systems left the Portishead branch at Ashton junction and after a set of long sidings it crossed over the river Avon on the Ashton swing bridge. This bridge was double decked, with the two railway lines below a public road. It was last swung in 1934 and was fixed in 1951; the lines were singled in 1976 and were rarely used after 1996. Weighing in at 1,000 tons, the hydraulically turned bridge was actually crossing the new Avon cut, built in 1809, when the floating harbour was constructed over the original course of the river.

After crossing the line to the Wapping cattle wharf the lines split between the two groups described above. Straight on, the track climbed over the junction locks, which protect the harbour during the very high tides that can cover the entrance lock. It then descended alongside the Merchants dock and curved around to rejoin the north side of the floating harbour before entering

A more general view of the remaining tracks along the south side of the harbour with inappropriate developments over the old coal sidings. (Author)

Canons Marsh. The depot had twenty-nine sidings at its peak, four of which were covered, plus extensions that ran to transit sheds, a timber yard and the gasworks. The branch was closed in 1964 and the entire area completely redeveloped; alas, little remains of its earlier life.

Today if we turn right after crossing the swing bridge, we join the Wapping wharf line, where the track is still in place, and then run along a narrow strip of land between the New Cut river and Cumberland Road. A sharp left turn takes us under the road and into the harbour area where we join the 1872 Bristol Harbour branch of the GWR. West from this point lies an extensive group of sidings used for coal distribution by the Western Fuel Company until 1987 and just beyond these is the Great Western Dock, home to *SS Great Britain*. The line now passes between loading wharfs and the massive Corporation of Bristol warehouses, today housing the Bristol Industrial Museum. Occasionally, the museum operates steam trains on this section of the old harbour network.

The lines then carried on eastwards, across the entrance to the Bathurst Basin and through the 292 yd long Redcliff tunnel under St Mary's church then into the small Redcliff goods depot, which worked until 1962. This last section closed in 1994, including the final run over Temple Gate and into the Temple Meads goods complex. All track east of St Mary's church is now completely buried under new roads and office blocks.

The Avonmouth area

There are just two lines now closed to passengers which feature Avonmouth and which just squeeze into what was originally Somerset and Avon. The oldest was opened in 1865 by the Bristol Port Railway & Pier Company and ran from Avonmouth south down the Avon Gorge to Hotwells (originally called Clifton until 1891), a strange terminus just short of the Clifton bridge. There was just one long platform with two more parallel lines, all three converging onto a turntable, which allowed the engine to be taken

The next station beyond the mile long Clifton tunnel is Sea Mills, seen here in the 1960s. (Lens of Sutton Association)

Avonmouth Dock station in 1960. The second platform on the right had been added in 1918 and the original wooden station building was rebuilt in brick in 1926. (Lens of Sutton Association)

A wagon belonging to the Bristol Docks specifically for use in Avonmouth. There would have been hundreds of such wagons in use around the dock system. (Author)

from the front of a newly arrived train, turned around and sent back via one of the two non platform lines to the front of its train. Once reliable tank engines arrived the turntable was removed and normal pointwork installed to form a simple run round loop. From here people would walk the remaining mile or so into Bristol alongside the river. Around 1870 when the docks were being built in Bristol along with the diversion for the river, the spoil was carried along the riverside road and up an incline (worked by a stationary steam engine), which crossed over the Port & Pier line just north of Hotwells. The spoil was used to fill in old quarries on Durdham Down.

Filton Junction station, looking northwards; the old line to Henbury and Avonmouth turned to the left in the distance. (Lens of Sutton Association)

Henbury station on the Avonmouth branch. This line was always best served by goods traffic, though today it is on the edge of Bristol's ever spreading development and could well make a return to passenger use. (Lens of Sutton Association)

In 1874 the Clifton Extension line, sponsored jointly by the GWR and the Midland Railway, reached Clifton Down station and, ten years and one long tunnel later, used the northern section of the Hotwells line to reach Avonmouth, carrying passengers from 1885. The tunnel was on a steep rising gradient (1 in 64) as it approached Clifton Down and, as the tunnel was usually full of smoke, a gong was fitted that was activated by the passing of the train to let the driver know he was about to leave the tunnel and enter the station. Midland goods trains used this route to leave Avonmouth and it was not unknown for the train to stall in the tunnel. The brakes were then pinned down, the train split into two sections, each hauled out of the tunnel and then re assembled in Clifton Down goods yard.

Passenger services on the little Hotwells line peaked in 1910 with ten weekday trains and six on Sundays, helped no doubt by the tramway which by then continued down the gorge towards Bristol centre. Immediately north of Hotwells were two short tunnels beyond which a second platform and passing loop were built in 1917, to handle the enormous number of munitions workers travelling to Avonmouth. Both the tramway and the Hotwells line disappeared beneath the A4 road built in 1921.

Our second line, opened in 1910 and still open for goods traffic, ran from Filton Junction to Avonmouth, the last couple of miles using the Severn Beach line. This was built partly to solve the problem of LMS goods trains having to use the Clifton Down route. Between Charlton and North Filton, the line passed between some of the assembly hangers and the runway of Filton airfield and a special crossing was built to allow aircraft to be towed across the line. It was put in originally in 1947 for the ill fated Brabazon aircraft.

The Filton Junction route was a GWR line, primarily for freight but it did have a regular weekday service (usually railmotors and later a GWR railcar) from Temple Meads of around six trains. Many of these ran a circular journey using the Clifton Down line from Avonmouth to return to Temple Meads. The Filton–Avonmouth line closed in 1965 along with the stations – Chittening Platform, Hallen Halt, Henbury, Charlton Halt and North Filton.

The Bristol & South Wales Union Railway

This grandly named company provides us with a very small but historically interesting section of long closed line. Opened in 1863, it built a single track broad gauge line from Bristol northwards to Pilning and to the New Passage Pier. From the pier it operated a ferry service across the Severn to Portskewett. On the now closed section there were stations at Pilning Low Level and New Passage plus a station at the end of the very substantial wooden pier. The line became part of the GWR in 1868 and was converted to standard gauge in 1873. A hotel had been erected near the pier with the usual Victorian enthusiasm for things new and novel.

Initially there was a service of six trains plus three on Sunday, which increased to eight with just two on Sunday by 1884. A

Severn Beach in the 1950s, looking towards New Passage and Pilning. Today only the left platform is used; the rest, including the station building, have all been built over. (Lens of Sutton Association)

New Passage Halt photographed on a somewhat dreary day, but showing how minimal were the facilities. (Stations UK)

siding had been added from New Passage to take coal to the pumping house being built for the new Severn tunnel, which opened in 1886 after a 13 year struggle. New Passage and the pier were now redundant and quickly fell into disrepair. The siding to the pump house was replaced when in 1900 a goods only line was opened from the line south-east of New Passage across the entrance to the Severn tunnel, then south-west along the river's edge and into the Avonmouth area. A station was built at Severn Beach with holidaymakers in mind and on the first weekend of passenger services in 1922, some 10,000 people arrived. A new siding was laid down to serve the pumping station, which continued to convey coal until the old beam engines were replaced by electric pumps in 1963. In 1928 New Passage Halt was opened not far from the defunct line to the old pier.

A passenger service commenced on the Severn Beach to Pilning section in 1928, with nine weekday trains and four on Sunday. These often ran as a circular trip from Bristol to Avonmouth, on through Severn Beach and back to Bristol via Pilning and Patchway. By the 1950s the numbers had dropped to five or six trains and many now only ran from Severn Beach to Pilning. Today trains still serve a very much reduced station at Severn Beach but the line to Pilning has completely disappeared.

7
Beware – Invaders

The Midland Railway
The other route from Bristol to Bath
The Thornbury branch

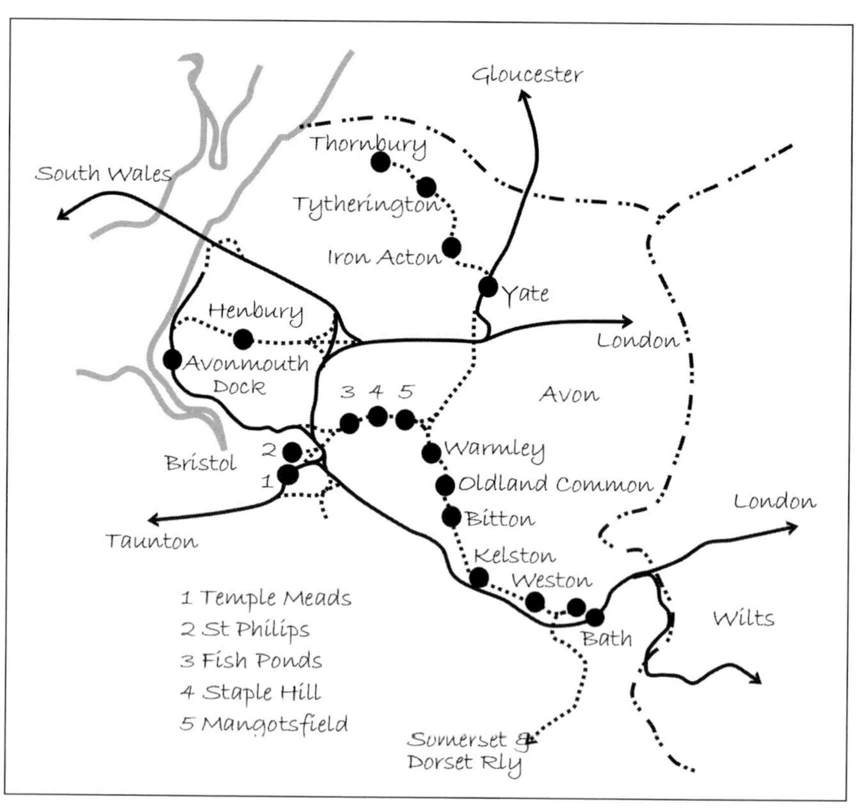

The Midland Railway

The origins of the Midland Railway in the area rest with the 1828 standard gauge, horse-drawn Bristol & Gloucestershire line built to convey coal and stone to Bristol Harbour. A branch, known as the Avon & Gloucestershire Railway, was built from near Mangotsfield to the river Avon at the behest of the Kennet & Avon Canal Company in 1831 whilst the 'main' line reached Bristol Avonside Wharf in 1835. The river Avon line closed around 1905. The Bristol & Gloucester Railway purchased the little horse-drawn line in the early 1840s and converted it to mixed broad and standard gauge (the Avon branch remained standard gauge). Just one year later it was purchased by the Midland Railway, which changed it all back to standard gauge in 1854.

Bristol St Philips was a small single platform terminus tucked away in the corner of a much bigger goods depot and engine shed complex. It was built around 1870 to relieve the pressure on the Temple Meads station. (E.T. Gill)

The route entered our area via Wickwar tunnel and Yate, west of Chipping Sodbury, from where, still heading south, it passed under the GWR London–Bristol line and into Mangotsfield before sweeping south-west through Fish Ponds and into Bristol. Its terminus in Bristol was originally Temple Meads but in 1870 its own station, St Philips, was built as Temple Meads had become very congested. Ironically, it was better situated to serve the city than Temple Meads, but with just one platform it was hardly a rival! In 1869 the Midland opened its branch line from Mangotsfield to Bath, which was later to become the feed from the north to the Somerset & Dorset system.

In 1874 a joint MR/GWR branch was opened to Clifton Down with the Midland feed coming via a short branch from just south

Avonmouth Dock station in 1932. As the docks expanded, the rail system and its stations changed many times. (Brunel University/Mowat Collection)

136

of Fish Ponds (Kingswood junction) and the GWR via a simple spur from its South Wales line. Later the line was extended through the mile long Clifton Down tunnel and onwards to Avonmouth. Connections between the Midland lines and the GWR system were put in virtually everywhere the two companies crossed, emphasising that the GWR didn't see the Midland as a serious competitor, unlike its arch rival the LSWR.

The Midland service from Fish Ponds to Clifton Down saw up to 13 trains on weekdays, some running from Fish Ponds, some from Mangotsfield and some from Bath.

The Midland Railway terminus at St Philips station was a very modest affair with just one platform tucked away in the corner of a vast goods depot. Moving across yet more sidings from the terminus was the Barrow Road engine shed.

From the centre of this maze a double line emerged, which dropped the short distance to serve a riverside wharf – following the original horse-drawn route. The wharf was squeezed into a small area but nevertheless served many local industries plus a fleet of 120 ton barges that could access the entire floating harbour area where virtually all of Bristol's early industry was situated. To allow for cargoes that had to be kept dry a 160 ft long canopy was built. The tight curves and pointwork of these lines meant work for small locomotives, latterly former Lancashire and Yorkshire 0-4-0 'pugs' and class 3 diesels. In 1985 this line was used to serve a modern refuse transfer station though the riverside area still had other factories including a Blue Circle cement depot. Alas, this part of the old goods system closed in 1990.

The other route from Bristol to Bath

When the Midland arrived in Bristol in 1845 it wasted no time in announcing its intention to build a branch to Bath. As usual several schemes came and went, including a suggestion in 1863 from the Bath City Council that the line should join the existing GWR line near Saltford and have running powers into the GWR

Fish Ponds station was the first station out of Bristol on the old LMS Gloucester route. Here a pannier-headed enthusiasts' special awaits its next move. (E.T. Gill)

station. Though the GWR would have none of this, the simple fact was that the GWR station was incapable of being expanded to handle the extra traffic. Eventually in 1864 the Act was passed, though worries over flooding due to the proposed bridges, which crossed the river Avon six times downstream of Bath, continued. Construction set off at a good pace with some works being started before the necessary land had even been purchased! Mangotsfield station was moved nearer to Bristol so that it could serve both the Gloucester trains and the new Bath trains. The Midland had visions of passengers using this station to change trains rather than going into Temple Meads and duly built a surprisingly large station. The construction work complete, the line opened for business in August 1869.

It was basically a double track branch from the old Bristol–Gloucester line at Mangotsfield and headed south-east into the Avon valley, which it followed into Bath.

As we leave the Midland Railway terminus at St Philips on our journey for Bath we pass the Bristol Wagon Works, later to

Mangotsfield junction with the original Gloucester line nearest the camera. The Bath lines curve gently through the far platform, which was protected by the rather ugly windbreak boards. (Lens of Sutton Association)

Bitton station in 1906. A Johnson 0-4-4 locomotive is approaching with a train for Bristol. (Kidderminster Railway Museum)

Bitton station today, headquarters of the Avon Valley Railway. The buildings on the left hand platform remain almost unaltered despite the 100 year gap. (Author)

The northern junction at Mangotsfield in 1962 with a local train heading for Gloucester. The Carson's chocolate factory is in the distance on the left. (Millbrook House)

become the works and depot for the Bristol Tramways and Bus Company, still with rail connections until 1955. Next comes Kingswood junction where the Midland Railway link to the Clifton Down and Avonmouth line left by a junction facing Bath. On our right, at least up to the late 1950s, was a long siding originally put in to serve a local coal pit and later used for the Peckett locomotive works. Fish Ponds station, originally Stapleford then Fish Ponds, had an attractive group of buildings plus quite extensive goods facilities, which lasted until 1965. Next came Staple Hill station, a simple two platform commuter stop which simply couldn't compete with the electric trams that served this part of Bristol; trains ceased to stop here after 1940. The trackbed, including the 518 yd tunnel, is now part of a public footpath.

Mangotsfield station comes next, being the point at which the original Midland main line veered left to head northwards whilst the Bath branch swung south-east towards the Avon valley. The station sat in the 'Y' formed by the junction and appeared to be surprisingly large with glazed roofs held aloft on slender cast iron columns. The third side of the triangle was only used by through trains from the north heading to Bath; usually this meant trains destined for the Somerset & Dorset line. Oddly situated within the triangle was the large Carson's chocolate factory, which provided Mangotsfield station with many of its passengers.

Warmley station came next with a useful goods yard and a local brick and tile works, which generated traffic along with the Douglas motor cycle works in Kingswood. Ochre was also handled here, its red dust dominating the goods yard. All this area has coal near the surface – the story is told of workmen digging the subways at Mangotsfield being able to collect coal and again in the First World War coal was taken from the cuttings between Warmley and Bitton.

Oldland Common was a minor station with timber platforms and no points or signals. Today it is the northern terminus of the preserved Avon Valley railway, which operates from the next station, Bitton. This originally had a small goods yard and shed and is now full of collected artefacts typical of a young preserved steam railway. Apart from the inevitable coal, the yard here dealt

One of the six bridges over the Avon river. This is just before Kelston station. (Author)

Kelston station, which really served Saltford. The famous summer Saturday holiday expresses, heading for the Somerset & Dorset line, would pass this way. (Brunel University/Mowat Collection)

Weston station on the outskirts of Bath. Note the long walk to the up platform along the footpath. The penultimate Avon bridge was at the far end of the station. (Lens of Sutton Association)

with a wide variety of goods, including sheet steel, moulding sand, chemicals, hides and materials for a local paper mill.

We now move into the Avon river valley and reach the second of six bridges across the river, then Kelston station. The station was connected to the village by a mile long footpath; Saltford was much nearer but this was already well served by the GWR main line, so the MR line declined to mention it. Two bridges further on bring us to the outskirts of Bath and Weston station, which had several long sidings serving saw mills and a brewery. Again trams, this time from Bath, caused the trains not to stop after 1953. The rest of the journey is through considerable industry with gasometers, engine sheds and goods depots to the left and right. The Somerset & Dorset joined from the right and a siding to the left fed a chemical works and, after crossing the river, Bath gasworks. Coal for these works was important, with up to 40 wagons of coal arriving each day. Crossing the river Avon for the last time we enter the terminus in Bath Green Park station, sometimes referred to as Queen Square.

This station always features in books about the Somerset & Dorset line as it was here that the holiday trains arrived from the north via our branch. The train now had new crew and engines attached before setting off back towards Bristol then branching south and onto the gruelling gradients of the S&D. Green Park only had two platforms despite its grand overall roof, each having a run round loop giving four tracks down the centre. At the end of the north platform, there was a secure building into which vans carrying wines and spirits could be shunted. A crane then lowered the cases into a bonded cellar which ran under the entire length of the platform.

The local passenger service was always fairly good, starting with around nine trains in the 1870s and increasing slowly to around eighteen trains by 1910. Most used St Philips station in Bristol with the others running into Temple Meads. The Sunday service started with five trains and fell to just two but in the 1950s struggled back to five again. Locomotives were the usual Midland fare with Johnson 0-4-2 and 2P 0-4-4 tanks, plus 3P 4-4-0s and 2-4-0 tender locos. Ex-GWR diesel railcars plus push-pull working using diminutive 0-4-4s also featured into the 1950s. Heavier trains were handled by former LMS and BR 2-6-2 tanks and finally Hymek diesel hydraulics. Local passenger services were taken over by the inevitable DMUs.

Fortunately much of the line is now a pathway and the Avon Valley Railway at Bitton brings back the sounds and smells of a bygone age.

The original main Midland line from Gloucester had passed through Yate and then headed under the GWR lines before reaching Mangotsfield station. During the 1900s sidings were built north of Mangotsfield, near where the M4 passes overhead today, to relieve the congestion within Bristol's various goods yards. These slowly grew until there were some 25 sidings, but as traffic left the railways in the 1960s, they were closed in 1965. Just five years later the passenger services, using the old Midland lines, were diverted onto the GWR route south of Yate and the Mangotsfield line into Bristol was closed completely. There

Bath Green Park in 1963 with a Bristol train waiting to leave, behind a class 3, 2-6-2. The S&D trains usually used the right hand platform though both platforms have run round loops. The glass in the famous roof was lost in air raids and has never been replaced. (Kidderminster Railway Museum)

Today, thankfully, the structure still stands though it is now part of Sainsbury's car park. (Author)

was, however, still traffic to the old Avonside depot so a link was put in between the GWR South Wales line and the old St Philips/Avonside system. South of Mangotsfield coal was still being taken into Bath gasworks so the two Midland tracks south of Yate were used as two long sidings, one to the gasworks, the other used to train track maintenance staff. Alas, just one year later in 1971 the gasworks traffic ended but the old relief goods sidings were used again in 1985 to serve a refuse depot, and in 1990 when a Murco Petroleum terminal was opened.

Today the line has been converted into a public pathway for most of its journey. Bath Green Park station is now a car park for Sainsbury's and Bitton station hosts the Avon Valley steam railway. Not too bad for a line that closed to business over 35 years ago. The Avon Valley Railway has now extended towards Bath and operates steam trains to its new Avon Riverside station; eventually it hopes to reach the outskirts of Bath itself.

The Thornbury branch

This line may seem somewhat removed from Somerset but it was in fact within the Avon part of the Somerset and Avon 'county', so I hope you will forgive its inclusion!

Thornbury station in 1956. Today it is under a supermarket, a fate that has befallen the terminus of many a branch line. (Lens of Sutton Association)

Yate junction on the main Bristol to Gloucester line in 1932 with the Thornbury branch on the left. (Brunel University/Mowat Collection)

The first station was Iron Acton, with the truncated branch to Frampton on the left. (Brunel University/Mowat Collection)

The line was built to tap the iron, stone and coal workings around Frampton Cottrell and Iron Acton, both of which are within a couple of miles of Yate station. Opened in 1868, a year later it was extended to Tytherington and in 1872 Thornbury was reached. Two short tunnels were needed, one each side of the quarry. Thornbury boasted a proper stone built station but the halts at Iron Acton and Tytherington were humble wooden constructions. Unfortunately, the mine at Frampton closed just three years later, leaving a purely rural branch with a quarry near Tytherington (known as Grovesend) as the only source of goods traffic. For a couple of weeks in 1885 fortune did visit the line when a stranded whale at Littleton on the river Severn brought some 40,000 visitors, many walking the four miles from Thornbury station. In the 1940s ambulance trains of wounded soldiers were taken to Thornbury and the local hospital.

The quarry proved to be something of a saviour for the line and in 1955 a scheme was tried whereby the train of loaded wagons was to be drawn forward slowly, allowing an electric weighing machine to weigh each truck in turn as it passed over. The problem was that the line here is on a gradient of 1 in 64 and

Tytherington, with the little station in the distance in 1957. (Kidderminster Railway Museum)

A shot from just beyond Tytherington station today, showing the new track that was re-laid in 1972 when the quarry traffic restarted. The gradient looks frightening! (Author)

coupling the guard's van to the train was difficult, as was keeping the train moving slowly. Often the train would slide down the line to Tytherington station with some of the brakes on the wagons held down. The guard would then follow with any other trucks that were needed, using gravity and relying on the brake van's brakes to stop at the rear of the ballast train. On one occasion he left it too late, the brake van was smashed and the guard ended up in hospital.

Thornbury had a small wooden engine shed and the water supply came from a spring near the quarry, which was piped through the tunnel to Thornbury where it served the station, a local cold water bathing pool and the local sawmill.

Passenger traffic had always been light and the line closed to passengers in 1944, with goods lasting until 1967. The track was lifted and that might well have been the end but Amalgamated Roadstone was developing the quarry and wanted a rail link, so in 1972 the line was re-laid (using track from Mangotsfield). As so often, this revival was short-lived and by 1990 the traffic had ceased. Today the track remains with signs of an occasional train still running.

CONCLUSION

It is very easy to become sentimental about past times, carefully selecting those aspects that seem to us today to have been virtuous. The dramatic closures of railway lines in the 1950s and 60s will bring opinions varying from sadness to rage from the lips of railway enthusiasts, your author included. What hurts is not that progress is inevitable, but that a feature of our country was discarded so abruptly without any ceremony or thanks, and often with the suspicion of skulduggery.

What of course we forget is that the signs were there for decades before. Throughout this book I have been very conscious of writing phrases like 'traffic declined in the 1930s'. The end came to the branch line simply because the car and the lorry did the job better

Nevertheless, it would be quite wrong to underestimate the role that the local railways played for over a hundred years, enabling small towns and large villages to survive and prosper. It can seem amazing that in the early 20th century there were virtually no towns more than 15 miles from a railway – anywhere in England!

What I hope may have come as a surprise is just how busy and industrious Somerset was. Its lost railways covered the whole spectrum of services, from lazy old engines strolling across flat land with just one or two coaches, to massive double headed trains of twelve coaches packed with holidaymakers.

Today it is still possible to get a glimpse of the days of the steam railway in the preserved lines, Somerset's pride and joy being the West Somerset Line to Minehead, plus excellent smaller operations near Radstock and Bristol. As to the closed lines themselves, very little remains; some have become cycleways and footpaths, others are just suspicious dips in the fields or strange isolated embankments seeming to lead nowhere.

What of the future of railways? Today the remaining lines are subject to short-term accounting – make a profit or provide some easily measured benefit or close down. The current main line services are very good, often much better than the dreamed-of trains of yesteryear. Local services again are good and busy, though invariably dependent upon local subsidies. The network has remained relatively stable for many years despite the endless machinations of the politicians, and the future looks good. What often causes sighs of 'told you so' is that today many towns would benefit from a modern rail service if only their old, long closed lines had not been buried under new developments.

OPENING AND FINAL CLOSURE DATES OF LINES TO REGULAR PASSENGER TRAFFIC

Line	Opened	Final Closure
Yatton/Clevedon	28.7.1847	3.10.1966
Taunton/Yeovil	2.2.1856	15.6.1964
Burnham/Glastonbury	3.5.1858	29.10.1951
Shepton Mallet/Witham	9.11.1858	9.9.1963
Glastonbury/Wells	15.3.1859	29.10.1951
Glastonbury/Templecombe	3.2.1862	7.3.1966
Shepton Mallet/Wells	1.3.1862	9.9.1963
Taunton/Watchet	31.3.1862	4.1.1971
Hotwells/Avonmouth	6.3.1865	19. 9.1921
West Somerset Mineral Rly	4.9.1865	7.11.1898
Taunton/Chard	11.9.1866	10.9.1962
Bristol/Portishead	18.4.1867	7.9.1964
Chard Jn/Chard	8.5.1863	10.9.1962
Bristol/Bath(MR)	4.8.1869	7.3.1966
Yatton/Wells	5.4.1870	9.9.1963
Taunton/Barnstaple	1.11. 1873	3.10.1966
Yate/Thornbury	2. 9.1872	19.6.1944
Bristol/Radstock	3.9.1873	2.11.1959
Watchet/Minehead	16.7.1874	4.1.1971
Evercreech Jn/Bath	20.7. 1874	7.3.1966
Radstock/Frome	5.7.1875	2.11.1959
Hallatrow/Camerton	1.3.1882	21.9.1925
Bridgwater/Edington	21.7.1890	1.12.1952
Weston/Clevedon	1.12.1897	18.5.1940
Yatton/Blagdon	11.12.1901	14.9.1931
Clevedon/Portishead	7.8.1907	18.5.1940
Camerton/Limpley Stoke	9.5.1910	21.9.1925
Filton/Avonmouth	9.5.1910	5.7.1965
Severn Beach to Pilning	9.7.1928	23.11.1964

BIBLIOGRAPHY

Many books contribute to compiling a work such as this, some of
them adding just a snippet of information or a fleeting glance of
a site long gone. Of the following list a few are now out of print
but can sometimes be obtained secondhand.

Atthill, Robin *The Somerset & Dorset Railway* (David & Charles)
Harrison, J.D. *The Bridgwater Branch* (Oakwood Press)
Jackson, B.L. *Yeovil 150 Years of Railways* (Oakwood Press)
Maggs, Colin *Highbridge in its Heyday* (Oakwood Press)
Maggs, Colin *The Mangotsfield to Bath Line* (Oakwood Press)
Maggs, Colin *Branch Lines of Gloucestershire* (Alan Sutton)
Maggs, Colin *The Wrington Vale Light Railway* (Oakwood Press)
Mitchell, Vic & Smith, Keith *Branch Lines Around* series
    (Middleton Press)
Phillips, Derek *Working Yeovil to Taunton Steam* (Fox & Co)
Peters, Ivo *The Somerset and Dorset in the Fifties* (OPC)
Searle, Muriel *Lost Lines* (New Cavendish Books)
Smith, Peter *Footplate Over the Mendips* (OPC)
Vincent, Mike *Reflections on the Portishead Branch* (OPC)

INDEX